The Best Gay and Lesbian Films
(Glitter Awards, 2005)

compiled by Darwin Porter and Danforth Prince
Production, layout, and visual themes by Theodora Chowfatt

Blood Moon Productions
302A West 12th Street, #358
New York, NY 10014

www.BloodMoonProductions.com

Blood Moon Productions wishes to thank the press departments
and distributors of each of the films reviewed within this yearbook.
Especially appreciated are the Press and PR staffs at Cafe Entertainment
Studios, Fox Searchlight Films, Here! Films, Hollywood Independents, Lions
Gate Films, Norador Productions, Picture This! Entertainment, Screen Media
Ventures, Sony Pictures Classics, Strand Releasing, ThinkFilm, TLA
Releasing, Warner Independents, and Wolfe Releasing. To any filmmaker or
film distributor not mentioned in this list, please accept our sincere apologies.

LIVE FROM HOLLYWOOD

2005 Glitter Awards
THE INTERNATIONAL GAY FILM AWARDS

Texts and reviews by
Darwin Porter
and Danforth Prince.

Production, layout, and visual themes by
Theodora Chowfatt

Some of the most creative ideas in filmmaking have emerged from independent filmmakers. This book is dedicated to honoring their contribution to the creative context of gay and lesbian-sensitive moviemaking of films released during 2004, as recognized by THE 2005 GLITTER AWARDS.

What are the Glitter Awards?

The Glitter Awards celebrates, at yearly intervals, excellence in gay-themed films released during the previous year. Many, but not all, of the contenders were created through the verve and dedication of small-scale, lesser-known filmmakers, many with limited resources. Many of the nominated films enjoyed only a limited, and in some cases, very limited, showcasing in theaters. Consequently, many, despite positive reviews, were overlooked by the film industry's mainstream award shows.

Most of these films are strong in content, original in themes, and defiant of society's expectations. Cumulatively, they contribute enormously to the independent vision of filmmaking as it exists today. By changing the audience's perceptions of gay life, and enhancing the gay community's visibility worldwide through film, the films described within this guidebook have challenged people's ideas of what is normal and expected.

The Glitter Awards, often described as the Gay Oscars, hopes that this compilation of the year's best films will acknowledge the contribution of the filmmakers, their distributors and publicists, and the people who bring these stories to theaters. In the words of Jorge Ameer, founder of the annual Awards, "The name 'Glitter' was chosen because we believe that all of these films one way or another have had an impact on peoples' lives, and each deserves an opportunity to shine."

Within this yearbook, we've tried to convey some of the creative dilemmas faced by each of the filmmaking teams, and tried to describe their films with as much clarity and respect as possible. And although the winners are clearly designated, we hope that this book will help celebrate each of the nominated films and the teams who built them.

With apologies to those whose names were inadvertently omitted, and with regrets for anything which we might have misinterpreted, we salute independent filmmakers and their entourages, and wish them luck and strength in the challenges and adversities ahead.

For further information about the Glitter Awards, and submission of films for upcoming awards ceremonies, contact: The Glitter Awards, 1335 North La Brea, Suite 2197, Hollywood, CA 90028 (tel. 323/876-0975). **www.HollywoodIndependents.com.**

2005 Glitter Awards
Nominated Motion Pictures/Table of Contents

2005 Glitter Awards
Nominated Motion Pictures/Table of Contents

Winner, Best Picture:
Bad Education

Winner, Best Actor:
Gael Garcia Bernal in
Bad Education

Winner, Best Supporting Actor:
Peter Sarsgaard in *Kinsey*

Winner, Best Actress:
Laura Linney in
Kinsey

Winner, Best Supporting Actress:
Veronica Cartwright in
Straight Jacket

2005 GLITTER AWARD WINNERS

**Winner, Foreign
Film Festival
Award:**
Bad Education

**Winner,
Indie Film Award**
Brother to Brother

**Winner, Best
Documentary:**
Tarnation

**Winner, Gay
Press Award:**
Bad Education

**Winner, Best
Lesbian Feature:**
*My Mother Likes
Women*

Jorge Ameer

In times where our freedom of expression and artistry are being threatened by the government with fines and crippling effects for "indecency laws," shows like the *Glitter Awards* are now more important than ever. Most, if not all, of these films could easily fall into the indecency category if the gay community continues to be targeted as the sacrificial lamb for the religious right. With such broad laws being enacted to restrict and impose morality, it is indispensable to keep the vision of creating images of hope, tolerance, human rights and dignity on our screens. Entertainment is the best way to reach and change the views of the general public. Communications arts and the media are the cornerstones of our society. They reflect images that set trends, lifestyles and the way of life as we know it. The images and experiences told through these films create an outlet for those who otherwise would be unable to find their lifestyle reflected in their surroundings. Within this "yearbook," we honor the releases of gay themed theatrical motion pictures. May our film community remain united in these trying times where our rights as artists are being challenged and threatened.

Jorge Ameer
Executive Director, The Glitter Awards

Against powerful odds, independent filmmaking with gay and lesbian overtones is a flourishing subculture in America today. Every year, the best of the GLBT genre is placed under the lens of The Glitter Awards, an annual showcase where the art form is celebrated and publicly acknowledged, and where awards are offered to those whose contributions to the field are exceptional and noteworthy.

Danforth Prince

Compiling this, the first of The Glitter Awards' annual yearbooks, has been a creative and gratifying challenge. We hope that it reflects the collective and individual genius of the filmmakers whose products were incorporated into its pages.

With apologies to anyone we inadvertently left out, and with the understanding that the format of this annual yearbook will adapt with the evolution of independent filmmaking, we thank the creative personalities who labored over these films.

Danforth Prince
President, Blood Moon Productions

WE WISH TO THANK THE
SPONSORS, ORGANIZATIONS, AND CELEBRITIES
WHO GRACIOUSLY BECAME ASSOCIATED
WITH THE 2005 GLITTER AWARD CEREMONIES

SPONSORS:
A.J. Productions, Advanced Video, Ariztical Entertainment,
Ascent Media, Avon Products, Birns & Sawyers,
Blood Moon Productions, Cake Divas, Cinema Source,
Divine HD-Voom, Erotic Museum of Hollywood, Filmthreat.com,
Frontiers Newsmagazine,
Hamburger Hamlet (6914 Hollywood Blvd, Hollywood),
Hollywood Independents,
IFP/West (now FIND-Film Independent),
Indiewire.com, The Knitting Factory, L.A. City Beat,
MIG Records, Steel City Productions,
Tequila Corazon, TLA Releasing,
Vanguard Cinema, Whalers Rum

HOSTS
Vicki Wagner and Miles Swain

AWARD MODEL
John Shaw

PRESENTERS:
Ryan Green, Vincent de Paul, Lacie Harmon,
Robin Greenspan, Jason Stuart, Mildred (a.k.a. Dred),

PERFORMERS:
Jason Stuart (www.jasonstuart.com),
Katia & Ksenia Aka Ru (www.migrecords.com),
Adrienne (www.migrecords.com),
Lotte Trouble (www.lottetrouble.com),
Quincy (quincysongs.com).

Frequently Asked Questions
about the Glitter Awards:

How is a film nominated for the Glitter Awards?
If a film has a substantial amount of gay and lesbian content, and if it enjoys a commercial theatrical release (i.e., a reasonable number of theaters agree to screen it, however briefly), and if it's NOT the product of one of Hollywood's large-scale film production studios, it's automatically included within the appropriate year's pool of nominated films.

Who are the judges for the year's Glitter Awards?
They include a loosely organized compendium of the program directors of Gay and Lesbian Film Festivals worldwide, and a loosely organized assortment of the publishers and entertainment editors of gay and lesbian publications worldwide.

Are DVD's of the 2005 Glitter Awards Ceremonies available for sale?
Yes, at film outlets and bookstores nationwide, or on the web at
www.vanguardcinema.com.

What are the dates for the 2006 Glitter Awards ceremony?
The Glitter Awards ceremonies are traditionally held on the Friday before the Sunday evening celebration of the Oscar Awards. The 2006 awards will be conducted in Los Angeles on March 3, 2006. For more information, click on
www.HollywoodIndependents.com.

What is Blood Moon Productions?
For more on that, and some of the other books we've published, turn to the final pages of this yearbook.

Adored: Diary of a Male Porn Star

PLOT SYNOPSIS:

After a long period of sepa-ration, Riki Kandinsky and his older brother, Federico, meet again at their father's funeral in France. Back at Riki's apartment in Rome, Federico learns that his brother is a male porn star. Shocked at first, he learns to accept his brother's lifestyle. The plot changes when Riki witnesses a car accident, leaving a beloved six-year-old tyke an orphan. Riki sets out to adopt the boy, fighting his grandparents in a bitter custody suit. The film ends on a tragic note when the legal action turns against Riki.

Written and directed by Marco Filiberti.
Released by Wolfe Releasing.
www.adoredthemovie.com
Genre: Drama
Runtime: 105 Minutes
Italian with English subtitles

The joy of sex and the diversity of family are celebrated in this movie, released in Italy as *Poco più di un anno fa*, or "A Little More Than a Year Ago." This dull title was obviously sensationalized for American release. To begin with, it is definitely not porn. Riki bears all but for hard-core action rent a DVD of one of those old Jeff Stryker releases. The film opened in key cities in America, mainly on the east and west coasts, but not in the red states, earning mixed reviews for Filiberti, and significantly a number of rave critiques.

Marco Filiberti

Filiberti cast himself as Riki Kandinsky. His stage name. His real name is Riccardo Soldani, the son of a bankrupt Italian nobleman. At the beginning of the movie, Riki is estranged from his family.

Upon the death of his father, Riki returns home for a dreaded but long overdue family reunion. Although Riki plays an internationally famous gay porn star, especially in Italy, his family is unaware of his profession. Obviously, none in the family is a devotee of porn.

At the funeral, he comes together with the co-star of the film, his brother Federico, as played by Urbano Barberini. After the funeral Riki's brother shows up in Rome where he is so shocked to see the picture of Riki on the cover of a porn magazine, he faints.

He's not so stunned by the news, however, that he fails to show up on the set of Riki's porn shoot the next day. Federico also feels the hard-rock bar concealed in Riki's underwear. Is Federico also a closeted gay? Even while pondering that thought, we learn otherwise. Federico falls for Rosalina Celentano, cast as Luna and playing Riki's agita-prone fag hag.

Filiberti portrays Riki in the words of one critic as a "*dolce vita* kind of guy who resembles a young Henry Winkler (that is so true) as a coiffed and cosmeticized actor created by Queen Nefertiti's makeup girl." In addition to Winkler, Riki also embodies one of those Luchino Visconti blonde fantasy figures, especially Helmut Berger or Bjord Andresen in *Death in Venice*. There's a lot of self-love in this film. Riki's bedroom is decorated with a giant poster of himself in a fetching pre-Raphaelite pose.

The film takes an abrupt turn when Riki witnesses the death of a lesbian mother in a traffic accident, leaving an adorable little dyke, Plapla, played by Edoardo Minciotti.

Feeling a paternal instinct, Riki wants to adopt the boy. Obviously he takes an uphill battle to gain custody, facing off against the boy's grandparents. As if we didn't know, society-at-large doesn't look with favor on male porn entertainers who dote on young boys (does that sound like a line from a made-for TV movie on Jacko?). In the film, incidentally, Riki's interest in Plapla is pure love, and not an attachment designed for pedophile pleasure.

The film is no *Boogie Nights*, but will interest many gay members of an international audience. Louis B. Mayer, being pitched this film idea by a scenario writer, might have asked: "Does it have a happy ending." Perhaps you've already answered that for yourself.

An Interview with Marco Filiberti

Question: Where did this character and story come from? And, why did you choose this for your first feature film?
Marco Filiberti: I wanted to tell of the encounter with the other self, with the other face of life and, above all, the desire for immortality, the desire to leave a mark of oneself that animates a somewhat normal boy...choosing the porno star was a direct, dispassionate way of associating these desires with a difficult character. It would have been too easy to talk of the personal search in an artist, even though this has been my obsession since childhood.

Q: Tell us about being Riki. Why did you want to play this character? Did you ever consider casting another actor and staying behind the camera, or just playing Riki and having someone else direct the film?
MF: I could talk about Riki for days. He is a mixture of harmonious contradictions: cheeky and discreet, deep and superficial, elegant and trashy, aristocratic and common, luminous and melancholic, generous and selfish. He's like an angel capable of lighting up the lives of others, but not his own, because he is still a prisoner of his own physique, the means by which he has used to impose himself upon the world, to shout his need to be loved. His feature is transversal. It's as if he were flying above things without letting himself be corrupted. The movie was born with him, while I was writing the movie I *became* Kandinsky...I assure you, I had no choice, I had to be Riki and the

father of Riki, in other words his director!

Q: Tell us about the other lead actors--Urbano Barberini, who plays Riki's brother, and Rosalinda Celentano, who plays Riki's friend Luna.

MF: I really wanted them. Urbano had all the characteristics to be Federico, he just had to release them, to pull them out. We worked hard together, and in the end became brothers, even though we are two completely different people. I believe he performed beautifully. It was different with Rosalinda; we already knew each other, we'd already worked together in my debut short. I had asked her if I could mold the character to her, and she said yes. Rosalinda is a poetic creature, somewhat of an inspiration for me...had she not played the role of Luna, I would have been forced to cut it. I believe that Luna is the double reflection of Riki, but as if sterilized, dried by the sexual bond.

Q: The porn industry is very different in Italy. It seems to practically be a part of mainstream pop culture, especially considering that a porn actress, Ciccolina, was elected to the national government at one point. Tell us more about the Italian porn industry and how you researched it for this film.

MF: In Italy, there was a porno star who really succeeded in becoming a myth: Moana Pozzi. In fact, when my movie came out, lots of people likened it to a male Moana. She too was elegant, luminous, totally void of vulgarity, and loved by the people. In Italy, the type of success described in the movie is very possible. As far as the industry is concerned, I can't say much. I have met a couple of directors and some actors, I visited a set...I have seen very diverse situations, some sets were very squalid, others much lighter, with nice kids who could have done any other kind of work. One of those I met (an American), suddenly quit and took up charity work.

Q: In person, you are a rather modest and soft-spoken gentleman. Was it challenging to play such a bold character who is literally adored by the masses?

MF: Making the decision to become a totally sincere artist was difficult, just as difficult as allowing the public to participate in my intimacy...Once I had understood that for me this work could not disregard this sort of public involvement I no longer had any problems. I gave Riki great chunks of myself and, after the movie, it was as if I had gotten rid of them. They are his now, not mine, not in that way however. A movie functions in this way too.

Urbano Barberini

Marco Filiberti

PRODUCTION CREW:

Director of Photography: Stefano Pancaldi
Editor: Valentina Girodo
Sound Department: Vittorio Melloni
Production Designer: Livia Borgognoni
Costume Designer: Eva Coen
Assistant Director: Paolo Borgato

WHAT THE CRITICS SAID:

"Scorching...A male porn star discovers the meaning of life."

Kevin Thomas *Los Angeles Times*

"Hauntingly erotic and dripping with romance."

Mike Szymanski *Tribune Media*

"Charming! A bold blend of heart and soul, camp, and sexual titillation into one engrossing tale."

Lawrence Ferber *The Advocate*

"Playfully erotic. Marco Filiberti captures the cosmopolitan, cheerful libertinism of porn in Italy. Lavishly shot and designed, another throwback to an era when directors like Roger Vadim and Radley Metzger, stylishly mixed sex, sets, risqué humor and melodrama."

Loren King *Planet Out*

CAST OF CHARACTERS

Marco Filiberti (Riki Kandinsky/Riccardo Soldani); Urbano Barberini (Federico Soldani); Alessandra Acciai (Juli); Rosalinda Celentano (Luna); Francesca d'Aloja (Charlotte); Erika Blanc (Angela Valle); Claudio Vanni (Claudio Alatri); Luigi Diberti (Rod Lariani/Porn Director); Caterina Cinieri (Silvio Valle); Giuliana Calandra (Franca Soldani); Franco Oppini (Gigi Ralli); Alberto Alemanno (First); Edoardo Minciotti (Plapla); Massimo Tellini (Guardian at the movies' archives)

Bad Education

Written and Directed by Pedro Almodóvar
Produced by Agustín Almodóvar
and Pedro Almodóvar
Released by Sony Pictures Classics
www.sonyclassics.com/badeducation
Genre: Drama/ Thriller
Runtime: 106 minutes
Spanish with English subtitles

PLOT SYNOPSIS:
Two kids, Enrique and Ignacio, discover love, cinema, and fear in a religious school at the start of the 60's. Father Manolo, the school principal and their literature teacher, is witness to and part of these discoveries. The three characters meet twice again, at the end of the 70's and 80's. The re-encounter will mark the life and death of some of them.

It is Madrid, 1980. Enrique Goded, a young and successful director of twenty-seven who, despite his youth, has already directed three successful films, is looking through the news in the tabloids for a story for his fourth film. One item in particular attracts his attention and he cuts it out: In a zoo in Taiwan, a woman threw herself into a pool full of crocodiles at a time of day when there was the greatest number of visitors. While the crocodiles were devouring her, the woman hugged one of them without making a sound.

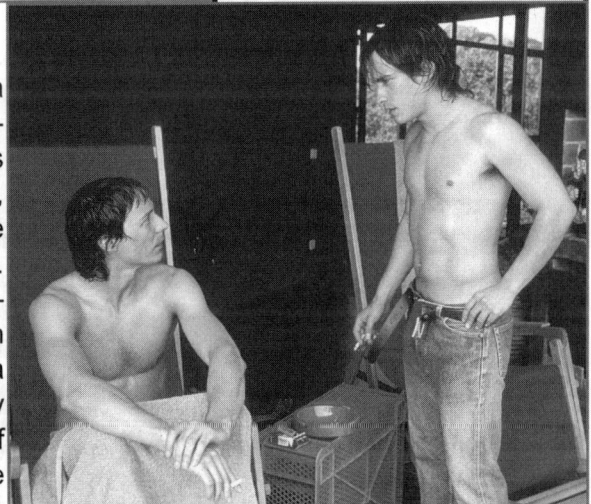
Fele Martinez and Gael Garcia Bernal

The doorbell rings. The visitor is an attractive young man with a beard who says he is an old school friend, Ignacio Rodríguez. Enrique remembers his school friend perfectly, but he doesn't recognize any of his features in the young visitor. But it's also true that they haven't seen each other for sixteen years. Enrique doesn't know it yet, but the story for his next film is in front of him, smiling and holding out his hand.

During their school days, Ignacio had a literary vocation, but he gradually gave it up for that of acting. In any case, he has brought a short story called *The Visit*. He gives it to Enrique in case it might interest him. The story was inspired by their childhood in school, their problems with priests--in paricular with the principal--the repression, the soccer games, the hypocrisy, the distortion of spirit, the harassment, and the masses sung in Latin by Ignacio who was the soloist in the choir. It also tells, in parallel, of an essential discovery for the two kids-- the cinema: Sara Montiel, *Hercules, Breakfast at*

Tiffany's, Moon River, Johnny Guitar, etc.
Within his short story, Ignacio has created a situation wherein the three characters--himself, Enrique, and the school principal--meet again, years later, when they are adults. Within the short story, Enrique has become a frustrated family man in the provinces, Father Manolo has left the Church, and Ignacio has become Zahara. Zahara is a drug addicted transvestite who impersonates Sara Montiel (a sort of Spanish gay icon of the '60s and '70s who vaguely resembles Mae West) and is a member of a fifth-rate variety company. The story is told from Zahara's point of view on the night she performs in the same city where Enrique and he/she went to school.

The re-encounter between the three characters, as depicted in the short story, ends tragically. Enrique reads it with great interest. He is moved by the first part, which deals with their childhood, in particular a love story with Ignacio, which was broken up by the closeted Father Manolo. In love with Ignacio, Father Manolo expells Enrique from the school so as to not have to compete with him for Ignacio's affections. The second part, when Ignacio (who has gone through a gender transformation and is now Zahara) re-visits the school disconcerts and fascinates him.

He decides to adapt *The Visit* into a film. When he tells Ignacio (who insists that Enrique call him by his current stage name, Ángel Andrade), the latter explodes with joy. He only imposes one condition: that he act in the film. Enrique doesn't mind, but when Ignacio (Ángel) insists on playing the lead, that is, the transvestite, Zahara, Enrique tells him that he isn't right for the character (neither does he understand the request). He is too masculine and too well built. Physically he isn't appropriate for a character like Zahara. But Ignacio (Ángel) insists, and demands that Enrique's trust. Enrique replies that he finds it very hard to trust him and they argue violently. Ignacio (Ángel) storms off in a fit of temper, insisting that if he doesn't play the role of Zahara, there won't be any film.

In the days following the argument, Enrique can't get the mystery visitor out of his mind. He investigates his characters in depth as a means of portraying them better--and discovers that the attractive boy who came to him to ask for work is not Ignacio Rodríguez but an imposter who had access to the real Ignacio, He also discovers that the real Ignacio died three years earlier, shortly after writing *The Visit*.

The shock of the discovery increases when, a few days later, Ángel Andrade (the false Ignacio) visits him again. He has shaved off his beard and slimmed down a little. Enrique thinks he has come to apologize and to explain everything, but it isn't so. The false Ignacio apologizes for the violent argument they had the last time they met, and offers Enrique the rights of *The Visit* to make a film of it without imposing any conditions.

Enrique doesn't say a word about the death of the real Ignacio, nor does he confront or accuse the impostor in any way. The impostor only asks to be allowed to audition for the role of Zahara. (Enrique listens to him in mute astonishment). But the false Ignacio (Ángel) has already lost weight, and since has also started working in a gay bar as a means of learning how to be a *queen*. Ángel is also receiving private lessons from Sandra, a transvestite who specializes in impersonating Sara Montiel.

Enrique auditions the false Ignacio, awards him the role of Zahara, and maneuvers him into becoming his lover/sex object. As part of a cat-and-mouse game, Enrique wants to know the imposter's reasons and how far he will go with his imposture. He also wants to know how Ignacio, his old school friend, died. He doesn't care what price he'll eventually have to pay for the adventure.

Long months of preparation go by. The first day of shooting on *The Visit* arrives, and eventually, so does the last one. Enrique penetrates Ángel Andrade frequently, but only physically. He doesn't manage to discover anything about Ignacio's death and Ángel's mystery remains intact. But on the last day of shooting, someone visits the set and hides behind the crew in order to see without being seen.

When Enrique goes back to his office to wrap up loose ends, he catches the mysterious stranger there, rummaging through his files. The visitor calls himself Mr. Berenguer, but Enrique recognizes Father Manolo, dressed in civilian clothes and seventeen years older than the last time he saw him, the day he expelled him from school. Now it is Enrique who expels him from his office. But Mr. Berenguer remains motionless and asks him: "Don't you want to know how Ignacio died and who killed him? Wouldn't you like to know the identity of the actor in your film?"

Driven by the same suicidal curiousity that led him to work with Ángel Andrade while knowing he was an imposter, Enrique lets Father Manolo tell him the true story of Ignacio-adult. As he listens, he feels like the woman who threw herself into the pool of crocodiles and hugged them while they ate her.

The famous and well-respected movie reviewer, Roger Ebert, simply gave up in trying to condense this movie plot. He finally tossed out that part of his review that attempted to summarize the convulted story line, claiming that *Bad Education* was a movie that "we are intended to wander around in." And so it is.

Almodóvar brings charm and grace to this *film noir*. Gael García Bernal shines brilliantly as the drag queen, and Fele Martínez as the director-writer is perhaps a quasi-autobiographical symbol for Almodóvar himself. A pretend Enrique is played convincingly by Raúl García Forniero, a young Ignacio by Nacho Pérez. Gleaming like a pedophile, Father Manolo is interpreted with razor-sharp finesse by Daniel Giménez Cacho.

Film-goers are left with a lot of puzzles to solve in this mystery. Of all the actors Gael García Bernal brings the same kind of dazzling screen presence that's evoked by an earlier Almodóvar dicovery, Antonio Banderas.

If your passion is for melodrama, and you adore role-playing, you've hooked up with the right film. In such a complex web of fantasy, illusion, and reality, you can lose control of what is actually happening. But somehow, that doesn't matter. The film is passionately involving.

WHAT THE CRITICS SAID:

"Combining in-your-face provocation with an ever increasing stylishness derived from classical Hollywood pictures and high fashion, Almodóvar has directed a film virtually every year. By his mid-forties he had reached a kind of maturity, turning from *enfant terrible* to accomplished maestro with a series of films that bring together formal brilliance, immaculate plotting, generosity of spirit, and emotional power."

Phillip French *The Observer*

"Cinematic maestro Pedro Almodóvar's ode to *film noir* can be seen as a consummate remake of his breathtaking 1987 film *The Law of Desire*. Both feature a film director (an Almodóvar stand-in) whose curiosity about a disturbed and beautiful young man (Antonia Banderas in *The Law of Desire* and Gael García Bernal in *Bad Education*) and passion for filmmaking are equated, but Almodóvar's ease and grace of expression have improved significantly with age."

H.K. *Premiere*

"Sex is a given in any Almodóvar movie, anyway. It's what [his] characters do. [But] his movies are never about sex, but about consequences and emotions. In *Bad Education*, he uses straight and gay (and for that matter, transvestite and transsexual) as categories which the "real" characters and the "fiction" characters use as roles, disguises, strategies, deceptions or simply as a way to make a living. There's no doubt in my mind that Almodóvar screened Alfred Hitchcock's *Vertigo* before making the movie and was fascinated with the idea of a man asking a woman to pretend to be the woman he loves, without knowing she actually *is* the woman he loves."

Roger Ebert

"Pedro Almodóvar has done it again. His new movie is a dizzying and rapturous *noir* melodrama, a little like Hitchcock's *Vertigo* with layers of confusion and contradiction. Perhaps it's not as powerful as his most recent film, *Talk to Her*, nor as extravagantly emotional as *All About My Mother*, but it is absorbing and playful and sensuous as only this director can be."

Peter Bradshaw *The Guardian*

"What is not a mystery is that the film lambasts the Catholic Church, not because the director was a victim of a pedophile, but for miseducation, sexual abuse of classmates, and for corporal punishment. One might add the church's support of the dictator Francisco Franco."

M.H. *Political Film Society*

WHAT THE CRITICS SAID (CONT'D):

"By setting the school scenes in the Franco era, Almodóvar explores a time when abuse by priests was even more hushed and terrifying than it is now. Scenes occurring in 1980 serve a different purpose. They allow Almodóvar's filmmaker counterpart to be young, sexually adventurous, and morally ambiguous. The director's naughty side emerges here, as if the gravity of the priest-abuse angle was too much to bear"

Carla Meyer *San Francisco Chronicle*

"While Almodóvar remains as fresh and as potent as ever visually and structurally, there's a distance in *Bad Education* that both beckons and repels. The movie examines fractured realities, but in trying to separate fact from fiction, Almodóvar loses the dramatic tug of his earlier efforts, *Talk to Her* and *All About My Mother*. This could be, in part, because the material is so close to Almodóvar"

Robert K. Elder *Tribune*

"*Bad Education* touches on the issues of dark double lives, the Catholic Church's abuse of their immense power, and pedophilia in the priesthood. The twists and turns in the story are too tedious and stilted, requiring too much work to follow. But there are few films that do such an admirable job of realistically depicting a life lived in response to the betrayal by the very person who should have been a trusted protector."

Joan Widdifield *Movie Magazine*

"Pedro Almodóvar doesn't just make movies. Almodóvar *is* the movies. He revels in everything forbidden and forgiving that can transform life into art. *Bad Education*, coming on the heels of the Spanish filmmaker's Oscar-winning *Talk to Her* and *All About My Mother*, is a rapturous masterwork. This story of two priest-abused boys who become lost men is also Almodóvar's most personal film to date--raw with his own feelings about sex, sin, the Catholic Church and the healing power of cinema. In one scene, the pubescent boys go to a movie house and jerk each other off while watching Spanish sex icon Sarita Montiel. That's Almodóvar to a T: hand on crotch, eyes on a distant dream. "

Peter Travers *Rolling Stone*

"Pedro Almodóvar has toyed with film noir before, most memorably in his 1997 film *Live Flesh*. But his newest movie, *Bad Education,* is a delirious, headlong immersion and re-invention of a style that has lured countless filmmakers onto its treacherous shoals. Because we live in a shameless age, this genre--synonymous with secrets, shadows, and twisty, hairpin-turning plots that point toward an abyss--often seems forced when its conventions are recycled in our tell all tabloid environment."

Stephen Holden *The New York Times*

Director's Comments: Pedro Almodóvar

"I had to make *Bad Education*. I had to get it out of my system before it became an obsession. I had worked repeatedly on the script for over ten years and I could have gone on like that for another ten decades. Because of the amount of possible combinations, the story of *Bad Education* was only finished once the film had been shot, edited, and mixed.

Bad Education is a very intimate film, but not exactly autobiographical. I mean that I'm not recounting my life at school or all that I lived and learned during the first years of the *movida*, although those are two periods in which the story is set (1964 and 1980, with an interval in 1977). Of course my memories were important when it came to writing the script. After all, I lived in the setting and in the periods in which it takes place.

Bad Education is not a settling of scores with the priests who "bad-educated" me or with the clergy in general. If I had needed to take revenge I wouldn't have waited forty years to do so. The church doesn't interest me, not even as an adversary.

Nor is the film a reflection on the *movida* in Madrid at the start of the '80s, even though a large part of it is set in Madrid of that time. What interests me about that historic moment is the explosion of freedom that Spain was experiencing, as opposed to the obscurantism and repression of the '60s. The early '80s are, therefore, the ideal setting for protagonists, now adults, to be masters of their own destinies, their bodies and their desires.

The film is not a comedy, although there is humor (Javier Cámara's character), nor is it a children's musical although there are children singing. It is a "film noir," or at least that is how I like to think of it.

The good thing about cinema, among many other things, is its capacity to convert into spectacle and entertainment the worst of our nature."

Fele Martínez

Gael García Bernal

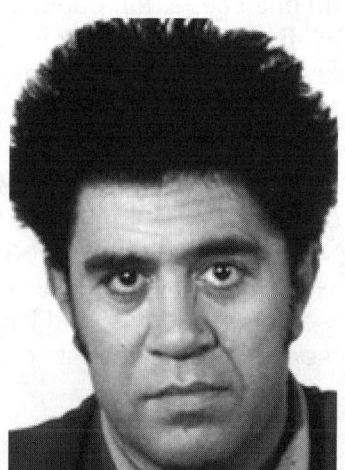
Pedro Almodóvar

Who's Who in the Cast

Gael García Bernal- Born in Mexico to actor parents, Gael became familiar with the world of acting from a very early age. Since beginning his career in television in the series *Teresa*, he has participated in many productions in various countries: Mexico, Spain, and England... He studied at the Central School of Speech and Drama in London. His most remarkable films include *Amores Perros* (Alejandro González-Iñárritu), *No News From God* (Agustin Diaz Yanes), *Y Tu Mama Tambien* (Alfonso Cuarón), *Vidas Privadas* (Fito Paez), *El Crimen del Padre Amaro (Carlos Carrera)* and *The Motorcycle Diaries.*

Fele Martínez- Born in Alicante, Spain, Fele Martínez is one of the most indispensible faces of "young Spanish cinema." He moved to Madrid where he trained at the Real Escuela Superior de Arte Dramático (Royal School of Dramatic Art) and then continued with a course in Antonio Madonna's Private School. He received the Goya Award for Best New Actor for *Thesis*, by Alejandro Almenábar in 1996. He has appeared in more than twenty films, the most notable of which, apart from the above, include: *Open Your Eyes* (Alejandro Almenábar), *Sleepless in Madrid* (Chus Gutiérrez), *The Lovers of the Artic Circle* (Julio Medem), *Black Tears* (Ricardo Franco), *April Captains* (María de Medeiros), *Talk to Her* (Pedro Almodóvar) and *Darkness* (Juame Balagueró). His latest adventure has been in theater, where he has successfully played Woody Allen's alter ego in the play *Play it Again, Sam.*

Daniel Giménez Cacho- Spanish by birth (Madrid), Daniel has managed to combine all kinds of acting work in his extensive career, from the theater, where he has acted in plays by Eugene O'Neill (*Long Day's Journey into Night*), Peter Nichols (*Passion Play*), Chesterton (*Double Face*), to lending his voice for the narrator in *Y Tu Mama Tambien*. He has worked for both famous and first-time directors on both sides of the Atlantic in more than thirty films. His filmography includes such notable titles as *Chronos* (Guillermo del Toro), *Miracle Alley* (Jorge Fons), *Nobody Will Speak of Us When We're Dead* (Agustín Díaz Yanes), *Deep Crimson* (Arturo Ripstein), and *Jealousy* (Vicente Aranda).

Javier Cámara- Javier Cámara was born in La Rioja and came to Madrid to study acting at the Real Escuela Superior de Arte Dramático (Royal School of Dramatic Art). Since then, he has worked in all the media possible for an actor: Theater, film, and television. His various roles have won him great popularity among audiences in various countries. His most notable work includes that of the protagonist in *Talk to Her* (Pedro Almodóvar) which brought him international recognition and for which he recieved the Audience Award for the Best European Actor of 2002. Since making his debut in *Alegre ma non troppo* (Fernando Colomo), he has managed to become one of the best loved actors in films such as *Torrente, the Stupid Arm of the Law* (Santiago Segura), *Torremolinos 73* (Pablo Berger), *Los abajos firmantes* (Joaquín Oristrell) and in the television series *Ay, señor, señor!* and *Siete vidas.*

Who's Who in the Cast (cont'd)

Lluís Homar- Born in Barcelona, Lluís has been able to combine theater, to which he has dedicated most of his extensive career, with cinema and television. He studied law at the Autonomous University in Barcelona after which he completed several acting courses: Uta Hagen (1986-87) in New York and John Strasberg (1985) among others. He was one of the founders of the Teatre Lilure and its director from 1992-1998. He has acted in and directed more than thirty theatrical works for this company. In 1999, he directed and starred in Shakespeare's *Hamlet* for the Grec Festival. Among the authors whose works he has directed and played on stage are David Mamet, Botho Strauss, and Ibsen. In cinema, he has worked for directors such as Pilar Miró, Vicente Aranda, and Mario Camus. In 1986, he received the National Acting Award. In 2000, he received the Fotogramas Silver Theater award for his portrayal of Hamlet.

Francisco Boira- Born in Huesca, Spain, he studied at Juan Carlos Corazza's Acting Studio. He has played supporting roles in important Spanish films such as *Morirás en Chafarinas*, by Pedro Olea, *Taxi*, by Carlos Saura, *Love Can Damage Your Health* by Pedro Gómez Pereira and *Novios* by Joaquín Oristrell. He has also collaborated successfully in the series *Todos los hombres sois iguales*.

CAST OF CHARACTERS

Gael García Bernal (Ángel/Juan/Zahara); Fele Martínez (Enrique Goded); Daniel Giménez Cacho (Father Manolo); Lluís Homar (Sr. Manuel Berenguer); Javier Cámara (Paca/Paquito); Petra Martínez (Mother); Nacho Peréz (Young Ignacio); Raúl García Forneiro (Young Enrique); Francisco Boira (Ignacio); Juan Fernández (Martín); Alberto Ferreiro (Enrique Serrano); Roberto Hoyas (Camarero); Francisco Maestre (Padre José); Leonor Watling (Mónica)

PRODUCTION CREW:

Director of Photography: José Salcedo
Executive Producer: Esther García
Music: Alberto Iglesias
Editor: José Salcedo
Costume Designers: Paco Delgado and Jean-Paul Gaultier

On Film Noir

Black are the priests' soutanes, black are the nights in the pupils' dormitory, black are the characters' destinies, and "noir" is the genre to which the story told in *Bad Education* belongs. Noir translates as "black," in French, in recognition of the country that rescued the genre, defined its identifying signs and encouraged its development as a major genre. *Film noir* (like almost all the noble genres) adapts easily to being mixed with other genres, provided the narrative has that breath of fatality without which black would be grey.

The noir genre mixes well with the melodrama in its toughest form (*Leave Her to Heaven* by John M. Stahl, *Mildred Pierce* by Michael Curtiz), with the most desperate romanticism (*Laura* by Preminger, *La Sirène du Mississippi* by Truffaut, *Out of the Past* by Jacques Tourneaur etc.), social criticism (Dashell Hammett, Raymond Chandler, James Ellroy, Vázquez Montalbán) or the terror-without-monsters, that is , the kind that comes straight from the human heart (*Human Desire*, in its two versions, Fritz Lang, whenever he works in this genre, *Fallen Angel* and *Angel Face* both by Preminger, etc.) or the meloncholy of the violent, if a genre can be assigned to this characteristic (Nicholas Ray: *A Lonely Place*, *On Dangerous Ground*). The noir genre even mixes well with the Western. Clint Eastwood's *Unforgiven* is really a thriller and *Mystic River* is really a Western.

In film noir there may not be policemen or guns or even physical violence, but there must be lies and fatality, qualities that are normally embodied by a woman: the *femme fatale*. The *femme fatale* (she isn't indispensible in the genre, but she is one of its great icons) is a woman aware of her power of seduction, hypo tense, so she won't be easily upset, who has lost her scruples and has no interest in recovering them. For her, sex is not a source of pleasure, but one of pain for everyone else.

In *Bad Education*, the *femme fatale* is an *enfant terrible*, the character played by Gael García Bernal, who strictly follows the example of Barbara Stanwyck, Jane Greer, Jean Simmons (*Angel Face*), Joan Bennett (*Scarlet Street*), Ann Dvorak, Mary Windsor, Lizabeth Scott, Veronica Lake, and so many other curses in the shape of a woman.

24

Interview With the Winner: Pedro Almodóvar

Question: In *Law of Desire* (1986) the transsexual played by Carmen Maura goes into the church of the school where she studied as a boy. She finds a priest playing the organ in the choir. The priest asks her who she is. Carmen confesses to him that she had been a pupil at the school and that he (the priest) had been in love with him. Is that the origin of *Bad Education*?

Pedro Almodóvar: More or less. Long before that, I had written a short story in which a transvestite goes back to the school where he had studied in order to blackmail the preists who had harassed him when he was a boy. While filming *Law of Desire* I remembered that story and it gave me the idea of Carmen's character going into the church at his school and meeting a priest who loved him when she was a boy. By then I was considering the idea of developing the story in detail. Carmen is a foreshadow of Zahara.

Q: There is also a film director in *Law of Desire*.

PA: Yes, and like Fele Martínez's character he mixes his personal desires with his work and in the end he pays a very high price for it. I've always been interested by the story of the artist who works with his own guts. It's fascinating adventure even if it never ends well.

Q: In your first statements you denied that the film was autobiographical.

PA: Paco Umbral says that everything that isn't autobiographical is plagiarism. The film is autobiographical but in a deeper sense. I am behind those characters but I'm not telling my life story.

Q: I believe you were a soloist in your school choir...

PA: Yes. And I sang all the time, masses in Latin, motets, etc. I sang at all the religious ceremonies and the celebrations. And I guess I didn't do too badly. The priests recorded some of the songs I sang and played them at the door of the church to attract the faithful. And I remember that we filled the church. I'd give anything to recover those tapes, but I don't think they exist. What i most enjoyed in my time at school were the religious ceremonies. I'm agnostic, but I think the Catholic liturgy has a dazzling richness, it fascinates me and moves me. But it's been a long time since I went to Mass. I don't know what it's like now.

Q: Does Father Manolo exist?

PA: Yes, as a character.

Q:But did he really exist?

PA: No. He's a made up character, although for some scenes I was inspired by two priests at school.

Q: For what scenes in particular?

PA: The harassment by the river and in the sacristy.

Q: Are they real scenes?
PA: Two schoolmates told me about them. If you're a boarder at a school you eventually find out about everything.

Q: If the two people who inspired Father Manolo are alive, aren't you afraid they might react?
PA: Admitting they were being alluded to would be like accusing themselves. I'm a director and a scriptwriter. For me, Father Manolo is a character, one with whom, I should mention in passing, I'm very satisfied. The character isn't a weapon thrown against the Catholic Church (which does have a lot of problems to solve, including its priests' sexuality. If celibacy didn't exist, there wouldn't be so many cases of abuse.) I didn't create Father Manolo and his prolongation, Mr. Berenguer, in order to attack the church. They are elements that allow me to talk about two of the many faces of passion. When Father Manolo is played by Daniel Giménez Cacho, the passion he feels for the boy, and his abuse of power, make him an executioner. When he calls himself Mr. Berenguer and has cast off his habits and falls in love with Juan, the same terrible character plays the opposite role in the roulette of passion. Now he is a victim. The film is inconceivable without those two characters, who are really one, and without their incarnation by Daniel Giménez Cacho and Lluís Homar respectively. Although, they are two veterans, they were two great discoveries for me. I can never thank them enough for their lack of prejudice, their depth and their unending willingness to satisy all the demands of a director as insatiable as I am.

Q: What can you tell me about the rest of the cast?
PA: They are suberb. Fele Martínez, Francisco Boira, the kids, Javier Cámara, Albero Ferreiro, Petra Martínez, Francisco Maestre, and, naturally Gael. It's admiracle to get it right with all the actors, especially when you don't know any of them, except Javier and Fele.

Q: Fele doesn't seem like himself, physically.
PA: I made him slim down and train for four or five months, until he got another (better) body, another physical attitude. He was delighted because everyone found him much sexier. As well as the physical aspect, we also worked on his tone of voice. I lowered its tessitura. He gave the character his heart, all of it, and his skin. I believe that from now on Fele will do other kinds of roles, less teen, more adult. He's an all-round actor. He can span the two extremes, torrid drama and crazy comedy. As happens in a different way with Javier Cámara. Javier is very versatile, he works in all the media (cinema, television, theater, cabaret) and in all genres. In *Talk to Her*, even though the role was dramatic, I discovered his gift for humor, and even though it's brief, his character in *Bad Education* was like an oasis for the whole crew. Javier is a comedic virtuoso. He has that special gift that goes beyond acting and can't be learned. His composition of *Paca* is rich, exhaustive, human, hilarious, dangerous for whoever is at his side because you only have eyes for him. A natural "scene-stealer."

Q: Poor Gael!
PA: Not in the slightest. Gael is going to work a lot and he's going to make lots of

money.

Q: How and why did you choose him, after cross-dressing every Spanish actor in the prime of young manhood?
PA: By auditioning him two or three times, like everyone else.

Q: What did he have that the others didn't?
PA: He was very attractive as a boy and a girl. And that was essential for under-standing his character's relationship with the others, the intensity with which every-one became obsessed with him.

Q: Is Gael the villain of the story?
PA: *Bad Education* is the opposite of a film with good guys and villains. In any case, I never judge characters whatever they do. My job is to represent them, explain them in all of their complexity and come up with an entertaining spectacle with all that. It isn't good for a film [when] the director judges his characters, even if they do atrocious things. Juan, the base-character that Gael plays, is a guy who doesn't stop at anything to achieve his ambitions. He is capable of killing, if the situation comes up, of seducing and of having sex with men and women, depending on his convenience. His absolute lack of scruples gives him an incredible strength, and makes of him a walking menace. But if you don't cross yourself in his ambition's path, Juan is a normal guy that can live perfectly integrated in society without anyone detecting the danger that he brings along. I like to compare it to Patricia Highsmith's amoral characters--Ripley, for example. Crime does not affect him morally, but ends up defining him. The character of Gael represents the typical *femme fatale* (in his case *enfant terrible*) because he leads all the characters who come in contact with him to their downfall. And *Downfall* is the Spanish title for *Double Indemnity* (by the genius Billy Wilder), noir among the noir-est, to which I am paying homage. Juan and Mr. Berenguer go to the Museum of Giant Figures in Valencia to plan a murder. Juan tells his lover that after they carry it out they mustn't see each other for a while. With the naivety of the typical manipulated lover, Mr. Berenguer thought that the murder would unite them forever but, on the contrary, it drives them apart and he can't bear that idea but it's too late to avoid it.

This scene is a reference to the scene in the supermarket in *Double Indemnity*. Even though I really like how it turned out, I'm aware that no film in color can sur-pass the image of Barbara Stanwyck in a curling blond wig and dark glasses, sur-rounded by stacks of canned food, all of it, including Fred MacMurray, in glorious black and white.

Q: What was it like working with Gael?
PA: A challenge, for him and for me. It isn't easy to play a character that is actually three, especially when two of them are vey different physically I guess it's the hard-est work that Gael has done to date. On top of the difficulty of changing sex and not looking grotesque, there was the accent. I wanted him to speak Spanish, not Mexican, which is very different...

Q: **The structure of *Bad Education* is at least as complicated as *Talk to Her*...**
PA: I think even more so. As in *Talk to Her*, in *Bad Education* there is a film within a film, but in this case it lasts half an hour, which is even more risky. Really, the film tells three stories, about three concentric triangles, which in the end turns out to be just one story.

Q: **The story of a director-scriptwriter loking for a story...**
PA: And who finds it. As Truman Capote said, quoting St. Teresa, "There are more tears shed over answered prayers than over unanswered prayers..."

The Many Faces of Gael Garcia Bernal

Gael Garcia Bernal as Zahara

Gael Garcia Bernal as Ernesto "Che" Guevara

Gael Garcia Bernal

Bear Cub
(Cachorro)

Written by Miguel Albaladejo
and Slavador Garcia Ruiz.
Directed by Miguel Albaladejo.
Produced by Juan Alexander
and José L. Garcia Arrojo.
Released by Star Line Productions/Hispanocine
Producciones Cinematograficas
in association with TLA Releasing.
www.medialuna-entertainment.de
Genre: Comedy/Drama
Runtime: 100 Minutes
Spanish with English subtitles

PLOT SYNOPSIS:
Pedro, a gay man with an active social life and a big circle of friends, takes his nephew Bernardo for a couple of weeks. When it appears as though it might become a permanent arrangement, however, Pedro turns to his friends for guidance as he and 9-year-old Bernardo begin to forge a household together.

Pedro is an attractive homosexual dentist, completely uninhibited in his relationships and with no feeling of responsibility to anyone but himself. He offers to take care of his 11 year-old nephew, Bernardo, while the child's mother, Pedro's older sister Violeta, still clinging to the outdated trappings of a hippie lifestyle, goes off to India with her latest boyfriend. Pedro has had very little previous contact, let alone any sort of relationship, with his nephew.

José Luis García Pérez

Pedro initially modifies his behaviour, not wanting his nephew to see what he is really like, nor the type of life he normally leads. The child, on the other hand, has a very normal attitude to things. He appears to be most at home. He is anything but a burden or a bother, and doesn't get in his uncle's way at all. Because of an unexpected twist, both their lives are transformed: Pedro learns that Violeta and her boyfriend have been arrested in India, and that Violeta will spend the next few years in prison there.

Pedro has to now rise to a series of unexpected challenges: (school, child upbringing, etc.). The relationship between uncle and nephew gradually becomes tighter and more solid, through real love, friendship and affection – things that Pedro had never really lived or experienced outside of himself. Everything is fine until Doña Teresa, Bernardo's paternal grandmother, appears on the scene, taking advantage of Violeta's absence to try to see her grandson. She homes in on the kid with emotional blackmail.

The upbringing of a child, she thinks, cannot be left to a homosexual.

Pedro, as played by José Luis Garcia Pérez, is a "bear" – and a gay bear at that. In case anyone out there didn't know, a "bear" is a big, hairy gay male, the very opposite of an emaciated metrosexual. Bears often like fellow bears, definitely not Calvin Klein underwear models.

The movie has heart, tackling such controversial issues as HIV and gay family life. Noting the title of the film, some reviewers cautioned against taking the kids to see it, thinking its an animal adventure, perhaps set in the Bronx Zoo. Admittedly, the drama opens with explicit sex between two men, and some scenes are a bit "hairy."
David Castillo as the very hip kid (Bernardo) steals this hirsute movie.

Arnold Schwarzenegger would approve of this Club; it's about burly men, not girlie men.

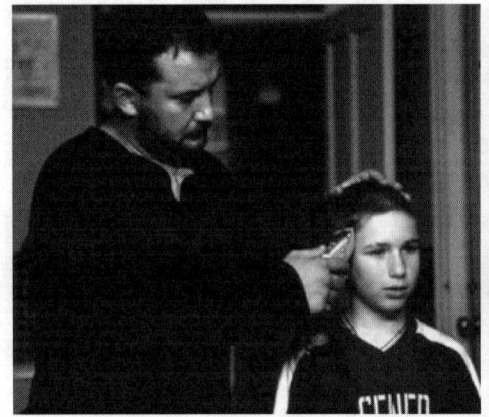

José Luis García Pérez and David Castillo

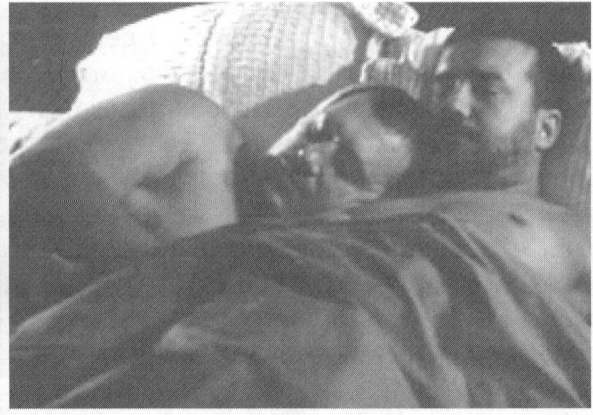

José Luis García Pérez and Arno Chevrier

PRODUCTION CREW:

Director of Photography: Alfonso Sanz
Music: Nacho Canut and Olvido Gara
Editor: Pablo Blanco
Production Management: Alicia Yubero
Sound Department: Patrick Ghislain

WHAT THE CRITICS SAID:

"In an early scene, a friend of Pedro comes to visit while Bernardo is there and pulls out a joint he very much intends to smoke. Pedro goes nuts and tells his buddy to stop. But he's only doing that because he assumes Bernardo will be horrified. The kid has no problem with it. He's seen it all before. This scene and other ones in the picture would likely be seen as examples of moral depravity by the ratings board of the Motion Picture Association of America and other deliberative bodies in the United States. But "Bear Cub" presents it all as matter-of-fact storytelling – something to deal with, morally speaking, but nothing to get sanctimoniously hysterical about."

Desson Thomson *Washington Post*

"*Bear Cub* moves deftly from a wry and affectionate father-son bonding comedy to a wrenching drama in which the uncle and the nephew's love for each other is put to the test. Castillo is a natural actor, and the versatile Garcia-Pérez takes an understated approach, which allows his portrayal of Pedro to accrue an impressive accumulative power."

Kevin Thomas and Kevin Crust *Los Angeles Times*

"Taking the seed of an idea and nurturing it into a fable about moral hypocrisy, *Bear Cub* substantiates prolific Spanish helmer Miguel Albaladejo's rep for well-observed, character-based dramas with an offbeat twist and a potent emotional undertow. A heartwarming take on a young boy's impact on the emotional life of a gay man, pic features no big names, but a dependable director and pic's unusual combination of explicit sex and unsensational treatment of off-limits subject-matter could lead to some European theatrical exposure, with screenings at gay-themed fests a certainty."

Jonathan Holland *Variety*

"How refreshing it is to see, for once, gay characters who don't look like buff, smooth Chelsea clones. How surprising to find a gay comedy that doesn't shy away from life's ugly, tawdry details. Yes, the men in bear cub are husky, burly, and proud."

Jorge Morales *Village Voice*

CAST OF CHARACTERS

José Luis García Pérez (Pedro); David Castillo (Bernardo); Empar Ferrer (Doña Teresa); Elvira Lindo (Violeta); Arno Chevrier (Manuel); Mario Arias (Javi); Josele Román (Gloria); Diana Cerezo (Lola); Daniel Llobregat (Bernardo, 14-years-old); Juanma Lara (Aitor); Jorge Calvo (Antonlo); Josep Tomás (Juan Carlos); Juanjo Martinez (Iván); Ramón Ramos (Ricardo); Patxi Uribarren (Quique)

WHAT THE CRITICS SAID (CONT'D):

"Spanish writer/director Miguel Albaladejo has beaten the odds with his film *Cachorro* (*Bear Cub*), a depiction of an unconventional modern family. While the usual sentimental suspects are all present and accounted for (abandoned child, father figure struggling with commitment issues, chronic illness), Albaladejo does a remarkable job of tempering the sweetness of his story with solid doses of acerbic wit and unabashed eroticism."

Jessica Reaves *Chicago Tribune*

"Albaladejo and co-screenwriter Salvador Garcia Ruiz take their film where few family dramas have dared to go. Pedro happens to be gay, HIV-positive and part of a subculture of gay men who call themselves bears because they let their body hair grow *au natural* and aren't obsessed with dieting or keeping toned. When they party together, it looks like a convention of Smokey Bears."

Ruthe Stein *San Francisco Chronicle*

"If *Bear Cub* were an American movie or television play, you can bet it would be puritanically wringing its hands over Pedro's supposed inappropriateness as a guardian and role model, not to mention the possible health risks Bernardo face living with an HIV-infected relative. It would probably involve a fierce court battle, a death scene and a final, tearful reunion between the son and his morally chastened mother. But *Bear Cub* calmly defies expectations at every turn. It opens with a fairly graphic gay threesome. It goes out of its way to portray HIV infection as something other than a death sentence. It also explores Pedro's relationship with a flight attendant and part-time love who wants a full-time commitment that Pedro in unwilling to make. It even follows Pedro to a gay bathhouse."

Stephen Holden *New York Times*

"There is amazing chemistry between the charming Pérez and the shining youngster Castillo. They form a new family unit that builds a wonderful emotional foundation for the film. Plus, Spanish director, Miguel Albaladejo, isn't shy about showing frisky sex, deep intimacy, and complicated human relationships. The film is never overly sentimental or sensational but is an amusingly touching film about reinterpreting the idea of "family" whether you are gay, straight, bear, or non-bear."

Lewis Tice *International Film Festival*

Bright Young Things

Directed by Stephen Fry who wrote the screen-play based on the novel by Evelyn Waugh.
Released by ThinkFilm.
www.brightyoungthingsthemovie.co.uk
Genre: Comedy/Drama
Runtime: 106 Minutes

PLOT SYNOPSIS:
This adaptation of Evelyn Waugh's brilliant novel, **Vile Bodies***, takes a penetrating and satirical look into the lives of the Paris Hiltons of yesterday, the beautiful, gild-ed, and sometimes Bright Young Things who "beauti-fied" England "between the wars."*

The characters in this movie live up to its title of *Bright Young Things*, being as bright as they are vile. The satirical film is a wicked and romantic romp based loosely on Evelyn Waugh's novel, *Vile Bodies*, original-ly published in 1930. When we first read the novel, we thought it one of the funniest ever written in English, an enjoyable piece of literature. Later we felt very lowbrow in our tastes when Waugh himself put down his own work, criticizing *Vile Bodies* for being "poorly construct-ed and second-hand."

Incidentally, Waugh's title of *Vile Bodies* had to go. Younger viewers thought the film might be about corpses or the living dead. The retitled *Bright Young Things* is set in that champagne-sipping era of debauchery known as England "between the wars."

Stephen Campbell Moore and
Emily Mortimer

Actor, writer, and first-time director Stephen Fry resisted the temptation to cast Paris Hilton in the film, although she was cited in almost every review as a spiritual sister in this tale of sex, scandal, and undeserved celebrity.

The film about the young, the rich, and the restless of the Jazz Age is not only engag-ing, but one of the most energetic of the past year. As their world hovers on the brink of a devastating war that will claim some of their lives, the Bright Young Things are par-tying themselves into exhaustion. In fact, one of the characters says, "What a lot of par-ties!"

On its simplest level, the film is about a dim, Candide-like hero, Adam Fenwick-Symes, as played by actor Stephen Campbell Moore. He wants to marry his lady love, the fra-grant, shallow, and flighty Nina Blunt (actress Emily Mortimer). Nina loves him--*yes, dah-ling I do*--but she detests poverty and needs a beau to marry her and support her in the style to which she is accustomed. Adam writes a novel to make money but it's seized by English customs as pornography, as he crosses from France to Dover. He is plunged into despair.

By a lucky break, Adam acquires a gossip column which becomes the source of his money. He's a friend of Lord Simon Balcairn, as played by James McAvoy. Simon is invited to all the best parties. Then as the columnist, "Mr. Chatterbox," he writes anonymous scandal about his fellow guests, a sort of Truman Capote betraying his rich friends in print.

Simon's society friends discover that he is double crossing them, and he doesn't get an invitation to the party of the year. He persuades Adam to stand in for him.

The Chatterbox column is printed in a newspaper owned by a Canadian press baron, Lord Monomark, a clever caricature of Lord Beaverbrook. Dan Aykroyd plays the press baron. His lordship is delighted with Adam's sensational, if not libelous, column and gives him the job of "Mr. Chatterbox." After hiring Adam, Lord Monomark says, "Ours is not to reason why, ours is but to poke and pry." With money in his pocket, Adam is still a long way from wedding Nina. Competing for her hand is Ginger Littlejohn, as played by David Tennant, a boring but monied mannequin.

The dialogue among the stars captures that lockjaw and facetious manner often used as a caricature of English aristocrats in the movies of the 1930s.

Supporting the leading roles are some of the finest actors now living (some of them only barely). Warhorses of yesterday are brought back to the screen. It's worth the price of admission to see the venerable 94-year-old Sir John Mills snorting cocaine through a straw--he might call it "naughty salt"--at a lavish society party.

The movie brings that glorious wreck of an actor, Peter O'Toole, back to the screen. When he's in camera range, no other actor has a chance of being noticed. He appears as Nina's old pater, Lord Blount.

The always glorious Stockard Channing appears as Mrs. Ape, a religious zealot arriving to convert the Bright Young Things, singing "Ain't No Flies on the Lamb of God." Her character is obviously based on that famous old evangelist of yesterday, Aimee Semple McPherson who has been impersonated in other films by other actresses.

Trivia note: the real Aimee is rumored to have taken the virginity of Ronald Reagan.

The costumes and the vintage cars are here, but movies containing those are plentiful. *Bright Young Things* has far more bite and polish than the regular run-of-the-mill *Great Gatsby* clone.

It is also ever so gay. Even when the characters aren't gay, they act that way. One reviewer cited "gay men flouncing as if Oscar Wilde had never been arrested."
What the viewer knows, and what the little lost lambs of the movie don't, is that their

lives are about to be changed forever with an oncoming war that will bring disaster to them and forever erase the trivial era they once occupied.

As long as Fry keeps the champagne flowing, he's on course with the film. He only gets maudlin when trying to deal with Waugh's moralizing.

Stephen Campbell Moore

Emily Mortimer

Dan Aykroyd

PRODUCTION CREW:

Director of Photography: Henry Braham
Art Direction: Lynne Huitson
Original Music: Anne Dudley
Casting: Wendy Brazington
Costumes: Nic Ede
Set Direction: Judy Farr
Production Designer: Michael Howells

WHAT THE CRITICS SAID:

"A delightful whirl of a movie that fizzes with energy and poignancy. Look out for sparkling cameos from Brit flick stalwarts."

Natasha Poliszczuk *InStyle*

"The renaissance man of British entertainment, Fry has captured all the anxious, frazzled spirit of Evelyn Waugh's novel *Vile Bodies* in an exhuberant directional debut. A polished affair, this star-studded social satire will appeal to the same sophisticated audience who journeyed to the cinema for *Gosford Park*. Breathless, fast paced, and very funny."

Allan Hunter *Screen International*

"Catapulted some 50 years into the age of neon and cocaine, the blithely uncaring junior British celebutantes who populate *Bright Young Things* might have found soul mates among the denizens of "Less than Zero." Both crowds party in brittle pursuit of whatever's trendy; both wreak casual but real emotional damage on one another. As such, "BYT" sweethearts Adam Symes (Stephen Campbell Moore) and Nina Blount (Emily Mortimer) fox-trot through a courtship dependent on the state of Adam's finances and ability to maintain Nina in the proto-Paris Hilton style to which she has become accustomed.

The screenplay for "Bright Young Things" is adapted from the great British satirist Evelyn Waugh's prescient 1930 novel "Vile Bodies," and both script and direction are the work of the glittering comedic polymath Stephen Fry. It's more difficult than ever, I think, to pull off a British period costume drama that doesn't look like it was unpacked from the mid-1980s "Masterpiece Theatre" circus trunk. Fry's sprightly attempt doesn't entirely avoid some of the clichés of drawing-room dramas actually set in drawing rooms, but his instincts are, happily, subversive. His cast is *crème de la Brit* (including Jim Broadbent, Imelda Staunton, Peter O'Toole, and 94-year-old John Mills). And Fry treats his bumbling characters--like the coarse Canadian publisher Lord Monomark (Dan Aykroyd) and the carny evangelist Mrs. Melrose Ape (Stockard Channing)--with contagious erupting glee."

Lisa Schwarzbaum *Entertainment Weekly*

"A delicious cocktail of glam costumes, eccentric characters and hilarious one-liners. This is a gem of a movie and a welcome treat."

Vishaka Read

WHAT THE CRITICS SAID (CONT'D):

"For its overall *joie-de-vivre* and a once-in-a-lifetime chance to see Sir John Mills snorting cocaine, *Bright Young Things* is strongly recommended."

GQ

"The story, with its quasi-farcical plot, may be nothing to write home about, or even pen a gossip column over, but "Bright Young Things" exults in its own giddy absurdity. Adam's social standing soars and plunges like the stock market, even with Nina, supposedly his romantic ally. She seems quite prepared to marry or drop him, depending on his money situation. And her bottom-line morality makes her very susceptible to the advances of Ginger Littlejohn (David Tennant), a childhood friend who has come into money.

When Nina sends Adam to ask her father for a loan, her hapless boyfriend finds himself face to face with the abrasively eccentric Col. Blount (Peter O'Toole). At first he mistreats Adam, mistaking him for a salesman. Then, after realizing his mistake, welcomes him and even writes him a fat check. Or does he? Adam discovers Col. Blount has a special trick up his sleeve.

Blount is one of several funny characters, including the elusive major and Agatha (Fenella Woolgar), a diehard party girl who finds herself, one hung-over morning, trying to breakfast with the disdainful prime minister (Bill Paterson). Agatha, you see, stayed over with the prime minister's partying daughter the night before; and now she's stuck making conversation with the priggish PM, with only her own flapper catchphrases and socialite ways to help her. It's a wonderful, disastrous encounter. Her clueless frivolity and increasing discomfort are divinely excruciating and, thanks to Fry's blithe spirit, discomforting fun."

Desson Thomson *Washington Post*

CAST OF CHARACTERS

Emily Mortimer (Nina Blount); Stephen Campbell Moore (Adam Fenwich-Symes); James McAvoy (Simon Balcairn); Michael Sheen (Miles); David Tennant (Ginger Littlejohn); Fenella Woolgar (Agatha); Dan Aykroyd (Lord Monomark); Jim Broadbent (Drunk Major); Simon Callow (King of Anatolia); Jim Carter (Chief Customs Officer); Stockard Channing (Mrs. Melrose Ape); Richard E. Grant (Father Rothschild); Julia McKenzie (Lottie Crump); John Mills (Man taking cocaine at party); Bill Paterson (Sir James Brown)

Brother to Brother

Written and directed by Rodney Evans.
Released by Wolfe Releasing.
www.brothertobrotherthemovie.com
Genre: Drama
Runtime: 94 Minutes

PLOT SYNOPSIS:
A drama that looks back on the Harlem Renaissance from the perspective of an elderly black writer who meets a gay teenager in a New York shelter for the homeless.

This heartfelt, fascinating, and absorbing film is a sensitive and entertaining journey into the sexual politics of the glory days now known as the "Harlem Renaissance" of the 1920s. This captivating drama that seesaws between modern times and the Roaring Twenties was both written and directed by Rodney Evans, an exciting new creator in filmmaking. His is one of the major cinematic debuts of the year, of special interest to gay black men. But its themes are universal, even holding intrigue for straight audiences if any of them will watch it.

Larry Gilliard Jr. and Anthony Mackie

The cast of skilled actors bring to life such legends as Langston Hughes, Zora Neale Hurston, James Baldwin, and Eldridge Cleaver in their youth. Some of these were the creators of the seminal literary journal, *Fire!*, that even angered the NAACP.

In the many "Cotton Club film depictions" of this stormy time in Harlem, *Brother to Brother* is the pioneering movie to deal with that era's vibrant gay and lesbian subculture. In both color and black-and-white sketches from yesterday, it brings back a time when Harlem was "full of scandalous parties peopled by good-time gals and queers."

Thrown out of his Brooklyn home by his homophobic father, Perry heads to Manhattan where he becomes a student at Columbia, working part-time at a homeless shelter. Along the way he looks for love in the form of a good-looking white male student, "Jim," as played by actor Alex Burns.

It's a bit of a stretch for Anthony Mackie, cast as Perry, to go from his role in Spike Lee's *She Hate Me* to this portrait of a sensitive gay artist in *Brother to Brother*. In the *She Hate Me* film, Mackie played a sperm-donor stud to half the lesbians in New York.

Described accurately as "young, gay, black, and beautiful" in the film, Perry goes to the homeless shelter after his classes. In both venues, he aspires to be something that he can't articulate. In the shelter he encounters an elderly Bruce Nugent, as brilliantly portrayed by Roger Robinson. Robinson deserves a standing ovation for his performance. "Young Bruce" is played in the film by Duane Boutte.

Nugent is a black gay poet who lived from 1906 to 1987. Through the eyes of this old man, the Harlem Renaissance lives anew. Nugent becomes Perry's guide not only back to the days of the Renaissance but as a role model on the virtues of an uncompromised life. It's a voyage of self-discovery for Perry.

Rounding out the cast, and doing so admirably, is Daniel Sunjata as Langston Hughes and Aunjanue Ellis as Zora Neale Hurston.

In spite of the film script's many successes, the drama piles a bit too much on the plate--black-on-black homophobia, light-skin versus dark-skin prejudice, and even writer's envy. Each of these subjects seemingly deserves a film development all on its own.

If the film cut is a bit too much to take in one sitting, we still applaud its ambition and its subject matter. We were especially captivated when Evans drew parallels with the problems of the past and how they tie in with African-American identity crises of today.

Duane Boutte

Anthony Mackie

Larry Gilliard Jr.

PRODUCTION CREW:

Director of Photography: Harlan Bosmajian
Art Direction: Claire Falkenberg and Nyna Sargent
Music: Marc Anthony Thompson
Editor: Sabine Hoffman
Casting: Tom Alberg, Vince Liebhart, and Ricki Maslar
Production Designer: Ernesto Solo
Costume Designer: Sarah Beers

Rodney Evans on Bringing Back the Harlem Renaissance

Brother to Brother is a project that I have been working on for the past six years. The idea for the script began when I started to think about different present-day experiences that I was having from a larger historical perspective. This led to my research into the Harlem Renaissance and Bruce Nugent at the Schomburg Library in Harlem. The more I learned about Nugent the more fascinated I became. Over the course of two years, I was awarded several residencies at various artist colonies around the country including Yaddo, Centrum and The Virginia Center for the Creative Arts. During this time period, I read a vast amount of material related to the Harlem Renaissance and completed several drafts of the script. Some of the historical material included "When Harlem Was in Vogue" by David Levering Lewis, Eric Garber's essay "A Spectacle in Color: The Lesbian and Gay Subculture of Jazz Age Harlem" and "Infants of The Spring" by Wallace Thurman. This is Thurman's autobiographical novel about the subversive artistic community that thrived in the house known as "Niggeratti Manor" which was the creative center for literary figures such as Langston Hughes, Bruce Nugent, and Zora Neale Hurston in the early stages of their careers. I also conducted several interviews with Thomas Wirth, a scholar of African-American literature, who gave me access to more than 30 hours of taped interviews with Bruce Nugent and an anthology of Bruce's art and writing. A great deal of this rich historical material was dramatized and incorporated into the script. The film draws parallels between the early phase of Bruce's life and the contemporary struggles of the younger, fictional character, Perry, who as young, gay, African-American artist has to grapple with similar issues of racism and homophobia in the present-day culture. The screenplay as it has been conceived is stylistically linked to the history of the African oral traditions and the methods and modes used to pass customs, traditions and experiences from one generation to the next. Another essential aspect of the script was that the form should mirror the complexity of Bruce Nugent's mind and his innate abililty to make connections between seemingly disparate ideas and events. The intimate personal relationships in the film also parallel larger social and cultural phenomena. As an example, the evolution of the relationship between the main characters, Bruce and Perry, runs parallel to the rise and fall of the "Niggeratti" and the Harlem Renaissance. The structure of the script is built around the gazes of Black men between each other in order to represent us (with all of our nuances and contradictions) as we really are.

Brother to Brother is the first feature-length narrative drama that deals with the rich cultural time period known as the Harlem Renaissance. It presents the lives and experiences of well-known writers such as Langston Hughes and Zora Neale Hurston who are read throughout the world and brings wider recognition to lesser known but equally important figures such as Bruce Nugent and Wallace Thurman. The film strives to make links between these historical figures and the lives of young, contemporary African-American artists of the Harlem Renaissance and the present day, I believe the quest for a meaningful identity and an original and truthful artistic voice is a universal theme that resonates on a global level. The film strives to acknowledge the diversity and complexity within the African-American and gay and lesbian communities and to give voice to experiences that have been vastly underrepresented in cinema for far too long.

CAST OF CHARACTERS

Anthony Mackie (Perry); Larry Gilliard Jr. (Marcus); Duane Boutte (Young Bruce); Daniel Sunjata (Langston); Alex Burns (Jim); Ray Ford (Wally); Aunjanue Ellis (Zora); Roger Robinson (Bruce Nugent); Brad Baily, Brian Everett Chandler, Kevin Jackson (Isaiah); Shantell Herndon, Billoah Greene, Ryan Michelle Bathe, Curtis L. McClarin (Rashan)

WHAT THE CRITICS SAID:

"Breathtaking...a fascinating and absorbing tale...heralds the emergence of an exciting new voice in black filmmaking."

Kirk Honeycutt *The Hollywood Reporter*

"A captivating drama...Tremendously accomplished filmmaking by writer/director Rodney Evans."

David Germain *The Associated Press*

"The story Evans tells of the spiritual link between a contemporary black gay New York artist and the trailblazers of the 1930's Harlem Renaissance is an exciting ambitious one, conveyed with guileless passion of purpose."

Owen Gleiberman *Entertainment Weekly*

"Excellent...a gifted cast brings to vibrant, sexy life the likes of Langston Hughes, Zora Neale Hurston, James Baldwin, and Eldridge Cleaver, and in the process conjures the neatest hat trick of all--making the loves and woes of the past resonate with those of the present."

Chuck Wilson *Los Angeles Weekly*

"One of the major cinematic debuts of the year...Anthony Mackie (8 Mile) emerges as one of the most talented actors of his generation; blazingly magnetic and calmly assured, Mackie gives full range to the inconsistencies and incongruities that make Perry's life so difficult. Perry's journey is more than a mere rite of passage, it is a terrifying blind leap into a more complex sense of oneself. In Mackie's hands, every discovery seems new and unique."

Gabriel Shanks *mixedreviews.net*

42

The Real Langston Hughes

Langston Hughes

Daniel Sunjata

The Real Zora Neale Hurston

Zora Neale Hurston

Aunjanue Ellis

Bulgarian Lovers
(Los Novios búlgaros)

Directed by Eloy de la Iglesia.
Written by Fernando Guillén Cuervo, Antonio Hens, Eloy de la Iglesia,
and Eduardo Mendicutti (novel).
Released by TLA Releasing.
www.tlareleasing.com/bulgarianlovers
Genre: Comedy/Drama
Runtime: 101 Minutes
Spanish with English subtitles

PLOT SYNOPSIS:
A splashy gay-themed story of a middle-aged Spanish man who falls in love with a newly arrived Bulgarian stud--he's supposedly straight and a hunk but predictably spells trouble. In the film, affluence, in the case of the Madrileño, grants a license to be a fool for love.

In this sex comedy and drama, Eloy de la Iglesia returns to the screen. He first won international acclaim with his *El Diputado* released in 1978, but that was a long time ago. He hasn't been seen since the 80s when he unleashed *Hidden Pleasures* and *Colegas* on the world. He's back and in good form in his first theatrical feature in years.

It's a love story...sort of, although the love is rather one sided. It's no secret that hundreds of refugees--both men and women--have fled from the former Eastern Bloc countries to the West in hopes of a better life. For gay men, especially older and affluent homosexuals, this has been

Dritan Biba and Fernando Guillén Cuervo

like winning lotto. For example, one traveler noted on a recent trip to Madrid, "I could have had my pick of at least a dozen handsome hunks, each of them from someplace outside of Spain, all for a reasonable price."

The pampered middle-aged narrator, and star, Daniel, as played convincingly by Fernando Guillén Cuervo, isn't adverse to preying on young and impoverished new arrivals in Madrid, especially if they are hot, handsome, and hung. He picks up Kyril (as played by Dritan Biba), a 23-year-old Bulgarian hottie. After checking out Daniel's apartment, Kyril proves to be a crude but effective lover, so much so that Daniel falls and falls hard. In Cuervo's performance, we have a virtual Spanish version of Kevin Spacey.

Daniel is backed up by his screaming queen best friend, Peón Nieto as Gildo.

Perhaps the funniest exchange in the film is when Daniel virtually falls before Kyril and claims, "I'd give my life for you." In response, Kyril informs him, "I'd also give your life for me."

Those who like their gay movies with graphic nudity, strong sexual content, racy language, and some drug use will find comfort here. As the plot deepens, Daniel learns that his hunk isn't adverse to stealing and smuggling--maybe and rather improbably a radioactive bag that Kyril stashes as Daniel's house. Daniel, blind with love, gets involved in Kyril's shady business affairs--yes, gangsters, drugs, even possibly radioactive materials.

Into this love nest emerges Kyril's girlfriend, arriving to come between the two male lovers. Anita Sinkovic is cast in the thankless role of Kyril's girlfriend, Kalina. Still in love, Daniel even pays for Kyril's wedding to his girlfriend in Bulgaria.

At the conclusion, even though Kyril has moved on, there is a younger relative of the hustler arriving in Madrid with his calculating eye set for Daniel. It's a case of "here we go again" or "falling in love again--I can't help it."

Fernando Guillén Cuervo

Anita Sinkovic, Fernando Guillén Cuervo, and Dritan Biba

PRODUCTION CREW:

Director of Photography: Néstor Calvo
Music: Antonio Meliveo
Editor: José Salcedo
Sound Department: Aitor Berenguer
Production Designer: Julio Torrecilla
Costume Designer: Pedro Moreno

WHAT THE CRITICS SAID:

"*Bulgarian Lovers* is sly, succinct--and very sexy. De la Iglesia has an ability to bring alive widely varying social milieus with wit and humor. The locales range from Madrid to Sofia, from gay clubs to a hilarious weekend in the country at Daniel's aristocratic parents' estate. The sensibility of *Bulgarian Lovers* is unmistakably gay, but its truths are universal."

Kevin Thomas *Los Angeles Times*

"Along with the romantic adventures experienced by Daniel, there's a message too: these immigrants to Spain are mostly ignored, except by the police, who harass them, and by men who are sexually interested in them."

Variety

"The gay sex scenes that punctuate Eloy de la Iglesia's limp Spanish comedy, Bulgarian Lovers, are frequent and graphic, and it often seems as if the lackluster story exists solely to showcase them."

Megan Lehmann *New York Post*

"Director de la Iglesia provides some stylish touches to the material, and the screenplay contains enough witty elements to lift it above the average sex farce."

Frank Scheck *The Hollywood Reporter*

CAST OF CHARACTERS

Fernando Guillén Cuervo (Daniel); Dritan Biba (Kyril); Pepón Nieto (Gildo); Roger Pera (Lawyer); Anita Sinkovic (Kalina); Fernando Albizu (Mogambo); Roman Luknár (Simeon); Simón Andreu (Daniel's father); Julia Martinez (Daniel's mother); Gracia Olayo (Rosita); Emma Penella (Remedios); Aure Sánchez (Bambi); Alberto Lozano (Taxista); Óscar Iniesta (Emil); Isabel Ampudia (Hermana 1)

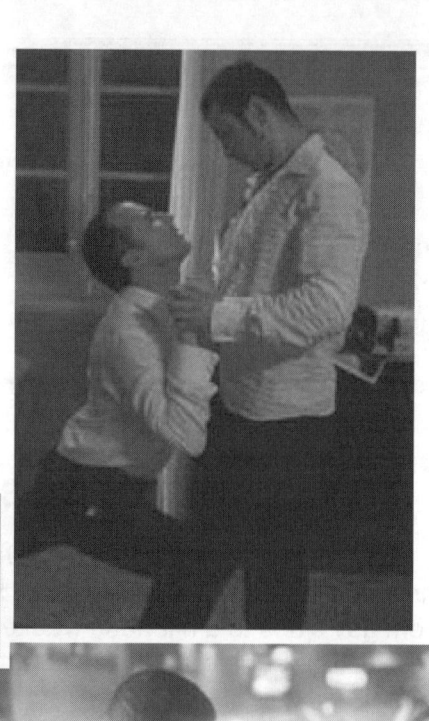

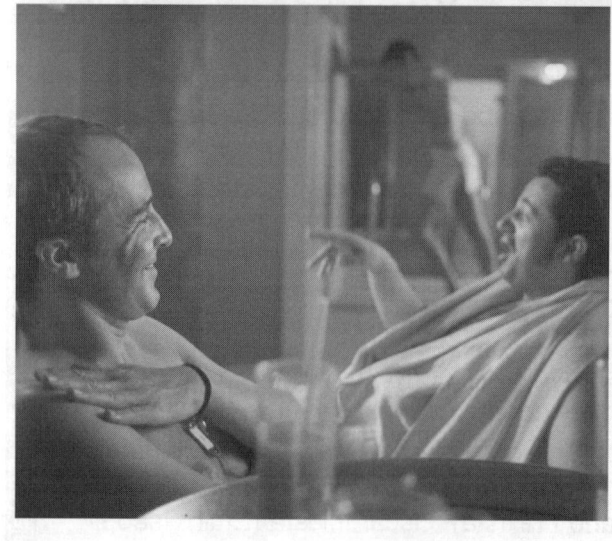

Callas Forever

Directed by Franco Zeffirelli and written by Zeffirelli, along with Martin Sherman. Co-produced by Medusa Film and Cattleya (Rome); Fil and General Productions (London), Galfin (Paris, Mediapro Pictures (Bucharest), and Alquimia Cinema (Madrid).
Released by Regent Releasing.
www.regentreleasing.com
Genre: Romance, Invented Biography
Runtime: 115 Minutes

PLOT SYNOPSIS:
A fictionalized account of the last days of opera diva Maria Callas. Determined to reignite her career, Jeremy Irons convinces Callas to film the opera **Carmen.**

"It's much easier to be worshipped than to be loved."
--Fanny Ardant commenting on the character of Maria Callas.

Callas Forever is arch, stylish, and stylized, and about a minute into its run, if you're gay and of a certain age, you'll realize that this is an "impressionistic sketch," or an aria, to remembered beauty. There's a demurely worded caveat at the end, acknowledging that the script

Gabriel Garko and Fanny Ardant

portrays Maria Callas as remembered by Franco Zeffirelli, and not necessarily as the historical figure she was. And from here, the film plays with your emotions, your sense of whimsy, your heartstrings, and your memory of what you thought you already knew about Callas.

The story line is a fictionalized account, a nostalgic "what if" tale, of what might have happened if circumstances had been different during the final year (1977) of Callas's life.

The plot requires the proposal and development, as part of the film, of a hypothetical arts venture which--because of Callas's extravagant (and perhaps overblown) sense of artistic integrity--eventually fails. And it fails despite the basic soundness of the reasoning behind the venture. Jeremy Irons plays musical entrepreneur Larry, perhaps as an autobiographical allegory for Zeffirelli himself. He's tired of developing an armada of rock and roll bands known for pissing on their audiences and destroying upscale hotel suites.

After picking up a new and handsome gay lover at the Paris airport, he bashes down the fortress doors of Callas's self-imposed isolation within her Paris apartment.

Once inside, he finds a feisty diva in a state of hugh dudgeon. She's drinking, popping pills, weeping uncontrollably and being an insomniac. She also lovingly picks up portraits of Aristotle Onassis, her only true love, and rages against Jacqueline Kennedy for stealing her man from her. She also obsessively plays long sections of her early recordings. In her failed voice, she mouths the words of her greatest successes.

Ever the diva, and perhaps secretly grateful that the dashing gay blade is still showing up after all these years, she berates him, mocks him, and finally, with more than a touch of what a psychiatrist might refer to as suppressed hysteria, embraces him and his commercial venture. Enabling and facilitating it all are the jolly ministrations of the outspoken, blowsy-looking English journalist and friend of the extended tribe, an Elsa Maxwell clone as engagingly played by Joan Plowright.

What's the venture? To expose a new generation of listeners to the artistic integrity of Maria Callas. Never having played *Carmen* on the stage, Callas will dress up in an embroidered mantilla, strut her stuff in front of a simulated cigar factory in Seville, emote like the vixen she can be, and lip-synch the words to recordings that she made of the Bizet opera back 20 years ago when her voice was in its prime.

Scads of good-looking corporate hipsters in the recording studio, thanks to Larry's salesmanship, grow intrigued with the idea, but only if *La Callas* will cooperate, behave, not throw too many of her legendary tantrums, and say nice things about the venture to the press.

Alas, it's too late. It's now 1977, and Callas's diva schtick and obsessive penchant for big hats and Chanel couture seem increasingly anachronistic. More important, Callas never really feels comfortable as a lip-synching drama queen. After scads of time and money (much of it Larry's) have been invested in the venue, she stages the kind of revolution that might have been inspired by the ending of Tosca itself. Like the heroine of Tosca, she commits (commercial) suicide, alienating investors, collaborators, and well-wishers in a grandly destructive gesture worthy of Medea herself. Her reasoning? Something high-blown, annoying, and linked to her unwillingness to compromise her standards of artistic integrity.

From that point, the film gets gauzy. Larry, despite the fact that he has lost a ton of money in the failed venture, clucks appreciatively and indulgently at the diva's point of view, retreats with his head bowed, ever the acquiescent servant. Callas, presumably, retreats to her Paris apartment with her recordings, like Norma Desmond in *Sunset Blvd*, to die. Society-watchers might be surprised that the film comments so little on her legendary relationship with Aristotle Onassis, and that it plays back only a snippet or two of film clips from the life and career of the real Callas.

One is left with the impression that only a very grand diva/director (Franco Zeffirelli) could ever have pulled off (and he did it with a lot of help from underlings) a campy film like this. At times it's absolutely fascinating, especially if you approach it with a previous appreciation for Callas, and especially if you happen to have been an upscale gay male living in Paris around the time of the diva's final years. Alas, those are esoteric standards indeed. Despite this films many intriguing virtues, even the French stayed away in droves, despite the winning performance of French-born actress Fanny Ardant, whose curriculum vitae includes many award-winning films as well as the real-life role as the former protégée of filmmaker François Truffaut. Her deftness at having captured the spirit of Callas, and the fact that she looks absolutely divine in all that Chanel, do a lot to make the film work.

Fanny Ardant

Gabriel Garko

Jeremy Irons

Fanny Ardant, and
Jeremy Irons

PRODUCTION CREW:

Director of Photography: Ennio Guarnieri
Art Direction: Carlo Centolavigna
Music: Alessio Vlad
Editor: Sean Barton
Production Managers: Gianluca Leurini and Marco Greco
Production Coordinator: Simona Battistelli
Script Supervisor: Angela Allen

WHAT THE CRITICS SAID:

"There's a kind of bent vampiric vibe to this film. On about five different levels, *Callas Forever* constitutes grave robbery. It's a big, honking, tutti-frutti sundae of a movie that nonetheless is shot through with authentic feeling. And it may be that there is no other way to capture what by all accounts was a tutti-frutti life."

Ty Burr *The Boston Globe*

"Dressed in Chanel from bedroom to boulevard, Ardent is every inch the diva. Aided by her uncanny resemblance to the singer, Ardent brings an energy and intelligence to the role that is totally convincing."

Judith Prescott *The Hollywood Reporter*

"Jeremy Irons' natural portrayal of Kelly's homosexuality is one of the film's most modern angles."

Deborah Young *Variety*

CAST OF CHARACTERS

Fanny Ardant (Maria Callas); Jeremy Irons (Larry Kelly); Joan Plowright (Sarah Keller); Jay Rodan (Michael); Gabriel Garko (Marco/Don José); Manuel De Blas (Esteban Gomez); Justino Diaz (Scarpia); Jean Dalric (Gerard); Anna Lelio (Bruna); Stephen Billington (Brendan); Alessandro Bertolucci (Marcello); Olivier Galfione (Thierry); Roberto Sanchez (Escamillo); Achille Brugnini (Ferruccio); Eugene Kohn (Eugene); Maria Del Mar Rivas (Frasquita); Concha Lopez (Mercedes)

Who Was Maria Callas? As If We Didn't Know

Born in New York of Greek parents in 1923, she's known as the most memorable opera singer of all time, not so much for the beauty of her voice as for the raw power and emotion she poured into her roles. (Ty Burr of the *Boston Globe* referred to her as "The Elvis of coloratura sopranos.")

Trained in Italy through the obsessive ministrations of her doting husband, G.B. Meneghini, she abandoned him in favor of a nine-year love affair with Aristotle Onassis. It was widely expected that they would marry ("the greatest Greek union since Ulysses with Penelope") but at the last minute, in 1968, Onassis abandoned her in favor of Jacqueline Kennedy.

Callas' ongoing grief over her loss of Onassis (he died in 1975; she followed him two years later at the relatively young age of 53) is today widely viewed as one of the key factors in her ailing health and increasing despondency.

For her admirers, the recordings of the roles she played (Norma, Ann Bolyn, Violetta, Elvira, and many others) are considered the definitive versions of musical characterizations which might never be surpassed.

Ironically, her cult-status fame reached its height at around the time her voice began to deteriorate. Critics almost universally cite the timing of her best performances as between 1949 and 1959. Some of these earned as many as 16 curtain calls, even from notoriously hard-to-please audiences in New York, London, Milan, and Rome. Callas-watching became a public spectator sport. Thanks partly to the quick pivots between her emotional highs and lows and her monumental, often tyrannical temper tantrums, commenting on the emotional binges of *La Callas* became one of the greatest games in the international arts community.

Her successes were epic and life-affirming. Her failures, including a disastrous operatic performance in Tokyo, were abysmal, and widely publicized in some cases, with the kind of venom usually associated with ancient Romans screaming for blood from gladiators in the Colisseum. For almost 30 years, she was the epitome of intense, highly dramatic glamor, storming her way across the stages of Europe, alternately terrorizing and delighting her colleagues and companions.

During the 1960s, as her voice deteriorated, she withdrew gradually from the stage, spending long weeks and months in seclusion in her apartment in Paris, popping pills and listening for long hours to recorded versions of her earlier artistry. Although she taught a series of master classes in New York in the early 1970s, and delivered a few scattered concerts as late as 1973-4, she gave her final full-length operatic performance at Covent Garden in 1965, playing the lead in Tosca.

The Real Maria Callas

Maria Callas

Fanny Ardant

In Memoriam: Maria Callas

Michelle Krisel, the artistic director of the Washington Opera, referred to Maria Callas as "the performer who changed the standard by which all opera singers are judged." Leonard Bernstein went further, describing Callas as "the greatest artist of the world." Italian musicologist Attila Csampai summed up her career, "During the ten years of her unquestioned reign, between 1949 and 1959, she bestowed upon the lost souls of the world - disoriented and bewildered by the after effects of World War II - more music, more art, more humanity and warmth than any other individual of this century."

The life and achievements of Maria Callas provided the raw materials for the film that was later produced and directed by Franco Zeffirelli, who was no stranger to high-blown operatic hyperbole of his own.

Carandiru

A Brazilian film by Hector Babenco.
Based on the book *Carandiru Station*
by Drauzio Varella.
Screenplay by Victor Navas, Hector Babenco,
and Fernando Bonassi.
Distributed by Sony Pictures Classics and HB
Filmes in association with Columbia TriStar do
Brasil, Globo Filmes, and BR Petrobras.
www.sonyclassics.com
Genre: Drama/Crime
Runtime: 153 Minutes
Portugese with English subtitles

PLOT SYNOPSIS:
A gritty Brazilian film based on the true-to-life experiences of Dr. Drauzio Varella inside the notorious state penitentiary, "Carandiru."

Set within the sweaty, high-pressure environment of Latin America's biggest prison, this is an epic, sprawling, and ambitious film that shows North American viewers a side to life in the Third World that they might never have otherwise even imagined. It was adapted from a Brazilian work of non-fiction (*Carandiru Station*).

Milton Cortaz, Sabotage, and Wagner Moura

The book's author, Brazilian oncologist Drauzio Varella, came late in his life to the world of book authorship.   He was already in his late 50s when his experiences as a volunteer in one of South America's biggest and roughest prisons (São Paulo's Casa de Detenção, also known as Carandiru) prompted him to record his experiences. It was his friendship, and his role as physician to noted Brazilian director Hector Babenco, that led to a commitment on the part of the director to make the film even before the book had been published. The filmmaking process brought together some of South America's finest actors and technicians, eventually attracting huge media attention within a nation that usually produces only a handful of films in any given year.

Gathering together the doctor's stories about life in Carandiru Prison, Babenco composed a sweeping tapestry that's loaded with pathos, humor, and a humanistic belief in the possibility of redemption.

The doctor, winningly played by a good-looking Danish-trained Brazilian actor named Louis Carlos Vasconcelos, is faced with horrendous problems inside this, Latin

55

America's largest jail: decaying facilities, diseases such as TV, leptospirosis, cachexia, and the beginning of a full-blown AIDS epidemic.   With more than 7,000 inmates and only rudimentary medical equipment, Carandiru is a huge challenge for the newly arrived doctor. But his work begins to bear fruit, and the doctor eventually earns the respect of the inmates. And with respect comes secrets, and his ability to deal with issues beyond disease.   The doctor's meetings with patients become "windows" into both the world of crime and into the sociology that's peculiar to the lives of the inmates.

Some of the most horrible insights are delivered at the quickest pace: The "yellow wing" houses rapists and informants, none of whom ever leave the musty premises of their prison-within-the-prison, even for exercise in the courtyard, because of the certainty of being knifed. What can and can't be done in Carandiru, and the punishment that's imposed in the event of any transgression, is not determined by the prison guards. The cellblock leaders do that. Cellblock leaders can gather the largest number of allies together, much as if they lived in a state of permanent feudal war.

At the film's end, when tensions and arbitrary feuds within the prison explode into a riot, army troops crash the gates, arbitrarily killing (through execution-style shootings in the head) more than a hundred of the inmates in a replication of an actual massacre. whose details were widely broadcast throughout Latin America in 1992.

Factoids about Carandiru Station--The Book

Drauzio Varella's *Estação Carandiru*, published by Companhia das Letras in 1999, represents one of the most successful sales phenomena in the history of Brazilian media, with sales in excess of 350,000 copies. It stayed on Brazil's bestseller list for 168 weeks.

Its genesis goes back to 1989, when Varella, who was born in the working-class Brás neighborhood of São Paulo, began his volunteer work as a doctor at the prison. A decade later, he recounted what he saw, with simplicity and generosity. By no means, at any time, did he set out "to renounce an antiquated and inhumane prison system." (This philosophy alone goes a long way in explaining why so many government agencies cooperated with Hector Babenco in the making of the film.)

Instead, Varella wanted to "individualize experiences within an environment where individuality does not count for much," and "bear witness to what I learned from the prisoners." In Varella's words, "*Estação Carandiru* is a collage of stories. The only historically accurate thing is the description of the massacre. This was narrated in the book in journalistic fashion, according to the prisoners' own exclusive version. I didn't add anything to what they told me. I summarized their accounts. When turning the book into a film, Hector merged characters and stories, and left some of them out. If Hector had wanted to narrate everything that's in the book, he would have made an eight-hour-long film. I know nothing about cinema. But I know that a film is a film, and a book is something else.

Carandiru--The Prison

The São Paulo House of Detention (Carandiru) was inaugurated in 1956 by then-mayor Jânio Quadros. The freedom that prisoners enjoyed within the film's depiction of Carandiru can be explained like this: Under Brazilian law, Carandiru was never officially designated as a penitentiary, but as a "detention house," a sort of entryway to the penal system. Into its confines were sent drug dealers, murders, and muggers prior to a trial and a formal conviction. With horrible consequences, many inmates remained incarcerated here for decades.

At Carandiru, every cell was decorated with its own paintings and depictions of saints, prayers, porn stars, and soccer players. Every convict, instead of following a unified standard, had his own rights and advantages, according to his power within the group. While the weak were forced to share a 90-square-foot cell with as many as 16 other prisoners, the strong lived in special suites.

In cells where as many as 17 prisoners lived, using the toilet between 7pm and 7am was forbidden, because of the discomfort brought by the smell to those who slept on the floor nearby. Even during the most intense heat, prisoners wore shirts during meals. Removing them was seen as bad manners. And during visitation days, no prisoner was allowed to gaze at another man's wife or girlfriend. When prisoners saw a woman, they usually bowed their heads down to show respect.

Forty-six years after its construction, on December 8, 2002, Governor Geraldo Alckmin personally ordered its implosion. Eight seconds were all that was required to turn the walls, common cells, and solitary confinement quarters into dust. The area that the prison occupied is now awaiting the construction of a leisure and cultural complex known as *Parque da Juventude* (*Youth Park*). Babenco's filmmaking team used eight cameras to film the implosion, images of which provide the film's conclusion.

Ailton Graça and
Maria Luísa Mendonça

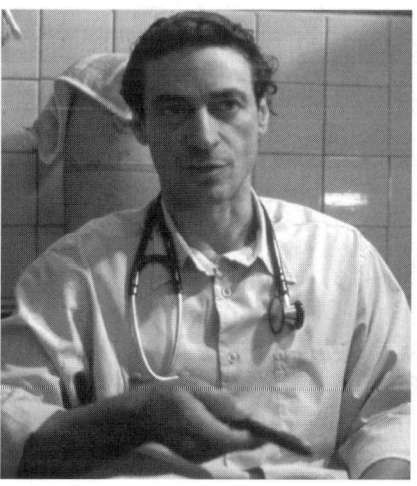

Luiz Carlos Vasconcelos

Rita Cadillac

PRODUCTION CREW:

Director of Photography: Walter Carvalho
Art Direction: Vera Hamburger
Music: André Abujamra
Casting: Vivian Golombek
Editor: Mauro Alice
Sound Department: Márcia Faria
Costume Designer: Cristina Camargo
Publicity Photos: Marlene Bergamo

WHAT THE CRITICS SAID:

"One watches it amazed, almost incredulous at the force and baroque detail of the violent stories of prison life and the vivid characters etched here. Yet the movie pulls you in and grips you."

Michael Wilmington

"Although less hip and sexy than *City of God*, Carandiru's bloody melodrama is at times electrifying. But, as we become immersed in the codes of the prison community, the film feels like a dysfunctional domestic drama, a telenovella with added weaponry--which, in fact, is not entirely a bad thing."

Wendy Ide

"Babenco gets a lot of mileage out of Christlike compositons, pinning a bullet-riddled inmate against a wall of metal bars as if on a crucifix. His real triumph, though, isn't in making us aware that *Carandiru's* prisoners were martyrs, but that they were human beings."

Michael O'Sullivan

CAST OF CHARACTERS

Luiz Carlos Vasconcelos (Physician); Milton Gonçalves (Seo Chico); Ivan de Almeida (Black Nigger); Ailton Graça (Highness); Maria Luisa Mendonça (Dalva); Aida Leiner (Rosirene); Rodrigo Santoro (Lady Di); Gero Camilo (No Way); Lázaro Ramos (Ezequiel); Caio Blat (Deusdete); Wagner Moura (Zico); Julia Ianina (Francineide); Sabrina Greve (Catarina); Floriano Peixoto (Antonio Carlos); Ricardo Blat (Claudiomiro); Vanessa Gerbelli (Célia); Leona Cavalli (Dina); Milhelm Cortaz (Dagger); Dionisio Neto (Lula); Antonio Grassi (St. Pires); Enrique Diaz (Gilson); Robson Nunes (Dadá); André Ceccato (Bristles); Bukassa, radio announcer (Detento); Sabotage (Weasles); Rita Cadillac (Rita Cadillac)

Carandiru--The Film

The production of *Carandiru*, from final script to first print and release, took three years, a technical team that included more than 250 professionals, and nine versions of the script, written jointly by Hector Babenco, Victor Navas, and Fernando Bonassi. The cast has 26 leading actors, 120 supporting actors, and 8,000 extras. Three months of arduous rehearsals prepared the 146 actors for their performance in the film. Although trained and paid actors played the roles of prisoners, makeup director Gabi Moraes had to reproduce more than 700 tattoos.

For the Carandiru Massacre sequence, more than 1,000 people were needed, along with six horses, six dogs, heavy weapons, and many gallons of fake blood.

The film features more than 40 different location sites, all of them in and around greater metropolitan São Paulo. The Carandiru scenes themselves were filmed in three different locations: at a smaller prison known as The Hippodrome Jail; Carandiru Prison itself, and in the studio. Construction of the studio sets required 12 weeks of hard labor and a construction crew of more than 150, as well as the support of both the Government of the State of São Paulo and the municipal government of São Bernardo do Campo. Filming consumed 600 cans of film, the equivalent of 45 miles of images. Editing of the film consumed eight months of work; sound editing required an additional four months. The mixing was done in New York City in five weeks.

Rodrigo Santoro and Gero Camilo

Who You're Likely to Meet in a Brazilian Jail

The film's narrative is like a jigsaw puzzle. One story fits into another to paint a realistic portrait (the filmmaker's words) of "the tragedy of Brazil." For reasons of brevity, filmmaker Babenco combined some of author Varella's characters together. But in the film version, archetypes you'd be likely to meet at Carandiru include the following.

1. *Black Nigger*--Swaggering, articulate, strong-armed, and shrewd, Ivan de Almeida functions as a kind of "judge" in the settlement of disputes among the inmates, administering a grim code of honor, transgressions for which is death. He has so many problems maintaining order in the jail that the doctor diagnoses his medical problem as equivalent to what's suffered by CEOs of major corporations: Stress.

2. *Zico and Deusdete*--inseparable friends since childhood, Zico (Wagner Moura) is at first the protector of Deusdete (Caio Blat), then his killer. In a fit of crack-induced dementia, he pours boiling water over Deusdete as he sleeps.

3. *The Beard*--Dangerous but offhanded, it's The Beard (André Ceccato) who says, "Anyone who says he doesn't have sex in here (with other inmates) is a liar."

4. *Lady Di*--A pre-operative transgendered person (Rodrigo Santoro) on the road to becoming female, he estimates his number of rectal intimacies in jail at around 2000. Amazingly, both he and his beloved, "*No Way*" (Gero Camilo), an inmate who learns enough about rudimentary medical procedures to act as the doctor's medical assistant), each tests negative on an AIDS screening test. Their nuptials are celebrated, lavishly, in jail, and later it is the demonstrative nature of their shared love that keeps them from being annihilated when their private cell is stormed by the Brazilian army.

5. *Highness*--We learn that Ailton Graça is the tough-minded survivor of multiple beatings with iron bars, yet he's no match for the combined fury of his two wives, Dalva (who's sexy and white) and Rosirene (who's sexy and black) when they meet, by accident, during days devoted to conjugal visits. Dalva is played by Maria Luísa Mendonça, Rosirene by Aida Leiner.

6. *Dagger*--a terse, tense, and utterly humorless hit man (Milhem Cortaz) with 39 murder convictions and some of the best tattoos in the film, he undergoes a noisy conversion to religion and becomes an evangelical priest.

7. Cohorts and bank robbers *Antonio Carlos* and *Claudiomiro* screw up a streak of winning bank heists with a disagreement over the cunning and deceitful Dina. Incarcerated together in Carandiru, they show a tenderness that's akin to romantic love. Floriano Peixoto plays Antonio Carlos; Ricardo Blat, Claudiomio, and Leona Cavalli, Dina.

8. Chief Warden *Señor Pires*--If any readers of this guide think they'd like to be abused by a sexy-looking authority figure (Antonio Grassi) with a baton, this is the man to do it.

9. *Old Chico*--Milton Gonçalves is obsessed with building miniature hot-air balloons, which usually ignite into flames before clearing the rooftops of Carandiru Prison. He has acquired wisdom during his sessions in solitary confinement, and is eventually released into the care of his 18 children.

Cowboys and Angels

Written and directed by David Gleeson.
Released by Media Luna Entertainment.
www.medialuna-entertainment.de
Genre: Drama/Comedy
Runtime: 89 Minutes

PLOT SYNOPSIS:
The story concerns a hapless civil servant who gets more than he bargained for when he moves into an apartment with a gay fashion student and finds himself on the catwalk. The film sets out to explore the difficulties for young people in keeping their identities in a fast moving culture of drugs and clubs.

Shane Butler is a handsome but geeky 20 year old who feels that life is passing him by. A talented artist who longs to go to Art School, he spends his days stuck in a horrible job behind a desk in the civil service. When he moves into an apartment in Ireland's Limerick City with Vincent Cusack, a gay fashion student, things begin to look up. Despite being poles apart on almost every level, Shane and Vincent soon become close friends.

Michael Legge

Vincent's artistry, evident in everything he puts his hand to, inspires Shane to greatness. When he meets and falls head over heels in love with Gemma, an ex-art student and best friend of Vincent's who now works in a fast food joint, he feels compelled to make some radical changes to his life.

Fate steps in to lend a hand in the form of Keith, a drug dealer who lives downstairs. Keith offers Shane the opportunity to make a lot of money by going on a drug run to Dublin. At first Shane refuses. But he desperately needs the cash.

He goes on the drug run and lives to regret it. With the money he has made Vincent transforms himself--"Pretty Woman" style--into one of the hippest cats in town. Unknown to Shane, though, some shady figures have tailed him back from Dublin and are now watching his apartment.

When Vincent finds out the source of Shane's cash they have a terrible confrontation which spells the end of their friendship. With the death of Shane's closest friend at work, Shane goes off the rails and plunges into an emotional abyss, culminating in an unforgettable night at the "Mud Club" after which Shane re-examines his whole life.

Shane renews his friendship with Vincent and helps him complete the collection for his graduate fashion show. At home that evening, celebrating their success, the police burst in and arrest both of them.

Convinced that this is the end of the road, Shane and Vincent are totally unaware of the forces conspiring to secure their release. When they march out of the police station, free men--with only hours to spare before Vincent's graduate fashion show--Vincent finally recognizes the new Shane for the mature and genuinely cool person he has become.

Never one to miss an opportunity, he uses Shane as his lead model on the catwalk. Shane is a natural and steals the show. Gemma finally falls for him. When Vincent flies off to New York to pursue a career in the fashion industry--with a ticket which Shane bought for him--Shane and Gemma are at the airport to say goodbye. The world has opened up for Shane now, and all he ever wanted from life is his for the taking.

This is a feel-good movie with the lead actors, Michael Legge and Allen Leech, showing some star potential here. All reviewers have compared it to *Queer Eye for the Straight Guy*. The two lead actors have a marvelous chemistry as mismatched roomies who work it all through to bond in the end. Those wanting the two male stars of the film to end up in the sack together, however, will be disappointed. It's platonic, baby.

This isn't really a so-called gay film, but a heartwarming "coming-of-age" story about two young men facing their challenges in modern day Ireland.

Amy Shiels

Michael Legge

Allen Leech

PRODUCTION CREW:

Director of Photography: Volker Tittel
Art Direction: David Doran
Music: Stephen McKeon
Casting: Gillian Reynolds
Editor: Andrew Bird
Costume Designer: Grania Preston

WHAT THE CRITICS SAID:

"The fact that *Cowboys & Angels* -- an odd-couple dramedy out of Ireland about the friendship between an awkward heterosexual civil servant (Michael Legge) and his gay, fashion-student roommate (Allen Leech) -- manages to avoid turning into either "Queer Eye for the Straight Guy" or a sexual-conversion story earns it two big points in the plus column. Otherwise, it's a sweet but slight film whose undeniable appeal is largely due to the performances of its flat-out adorable leads."

Michael O'Sullivan *Washington Post*

"From the pulsing opening montage of present-day Limerick, Gleeson's tyro work seems determined to upend a whole basketful of presumptions about the typical Irish film. No strumming harps or whistling Uilleann pipes intrude on Stephen McKeon's modern score, and no alluring grassy farmlands appear in Volker Tittel's sharp camera work. Everything that happens in "Cowboys' and Angels" indicates that nouveau Ireland is very much a part of the Euro mainstream."

Robert Koehler *Variety*

"David Gleeson's *Cowboys and Angels* takes an affectionate view of coming of age. Set in Ireland's picturesque Limerick City, this modest but fresh and appealing film reveals how two roommates, one straight, the other gay, affect each other."

Kevin Thomas *Los Angeles Times*

"While the film boasts few original elements, it does have its charms thanks to a witty screenplay that never takes itself too seriously and the endearing performances by its young leads. Butler ("Angela's Ashes") manages to make Shane appealing as well as geeky. Leech thankfully doesn't overdo his character's archness, and Shiels is alluring as the love interest."

Frank Scheck *The Hollywood Reporter*

"The characters are affable. And just as you're about to write off this modest film as unbelievably contrived (how often does a young man smoking his first joint get arrested for it--in his own home?), a welcome touch of humor or unexpected twist rounds the bend. The coming-of-age story about the corruptions of the big city has been done a few thousand times, but at least this one offers a fresh mix of open-minded intelligence and a heartfelt point of view."

Anita Gates *The New York Times*

CAST OF CHARACTERS

Michael Legge (Shane); Allen Leech (Vincent Cusack); Amy Shiels (Gemma); David Murray (Keith); Frank Kelly (Jerry); Colm Coogan (Budgie); Sean Power (Frankie); Alvaro Lucchesi (Bunny); Frank Coughlan (Richard)

Crutch

Directed and co-authored by Rob Moretti
(along with Paul Jacks as co-writer.)
Produced by Michael Anthony, Eric Smith,
and Rob Moretti.
Released by Illuminare Entertainment.
www.illuminare-ent.com
Genre: Drama
Runtime: 88 Minutes

PLOT SYNOPSIS:
Set in the suburban middle-class world outside New York City, this drama is based on the true life story of its director, Rob Moretti. It's about a student and his teacher crossing boundaries, and one of filmdom's most dysfunctional families.

Crutch is a dark and intensely personalized family drama that's based on a historical and autobiographical recitation of catastrophes from the filmmaker's childhood in suburban New Jersey. It transmits a belief in the premise that the exorcism of psychological demons can occur in the aftermath of a public disclosure of pain.

It's doubtful that anyone will see this without disturbing memories of his or her own Gothic childhood. More than

Rob Moretti and Eben Gordon

anything else, good writing and a red-hot performance from lead actor Eben Gordon keep viewers tuned to the nuances of this personalized exorcism of family-derived anguish.

Eben Gordon plays David, the cutest, brightest, and most talented 16-year-old in the history of the Garden State. Members of the audience are not the only ones who want to adopt him: The character of Kenny, skillfully portrayed by the film's writer, co-producer, and director, Rob Moretti, succeeds in actually maneuvering his way into legal custody of this brilliant but isolated teenager when his mother, foggy and in the throes of detox, signs over his care and custody.

Thirty-something Kenny, toxic and bitter, and unimpressed with his present gig as a method acting teacher in a public high school, has already "made it" in Hollywood, impressing his young pupils with his acting resumé, but never answering their query about why he has descended from Olympus for residency in the suburban hinterlands.

Emphasizing the fact that he's underaged, David is adorable as a teenager barely old enough to have a learner's permit. Their first kiss occurs after Kenny successfully navigates David through a driving lesson. Considering the 16-year-old's raw and surging talent, and the shit that seems to tumble down upon him from all sides, what red-blooded older gay male wouldn't develop a Lolito-obsession, reinforced by pride at having rescued the lad from his existential hell?

Kenny, as played by Moretti, is laser-eyed and jaw-droppingly handsome, pulling you into his orbit from the beginning. Early, he establishes himself as a beyond-jaded survivor of some of Hollywood's inner dramas. ("Acting--it brings lots of shit and very few rewards.")   Through something akin to laser vision (Rob does have beautiful eyes) coupled with the raw emotions conjured up during David's method acting classes, Kenny accurately deciphers the mechanics of David's suburban hell. Simultaneously, Maryanne (our favorite minor character within the film, see below) has laser-lights for Kenny and the dangerous liaison he's fostering with (jail bait) David.   Alas, Kenny's laser-lights only work one-directionally.   Kenny can accurately analyze David, but he can't analyze Maryanne, and he can't begin to analyze himself.

Whereas David's character grows more endearing as the film progresses, Kenny's grows meaner, more vindictive, and more spiteful. It's hard to believe that anyone as hip and good-looking as Rob Moretti can actually be as mean-spirited and narcissistic as the character he has called upon himself to play.   But by the end of the film, it's clear that Moretti had bigger fish to fry than simply making himself look good as an actor in his own film. His goal involved nothing less than a cinematic replay, and the subsequent exorcism, of his adolescent trauma.

The description of this family as an existentialist hell is reinforced by tearful revelations from David during the course of Kenny's acting class. David is first betrayed and then abandoned by everyone in the film, adding to his isolation. Later, the confessional tone of David's acting class is mirrored within the filmed confessions he makes to his 12-step encounter group. It is within the context of that setting, tempered with maturity and the passage of time, that some of the pain is washed away.

As voyeurs of someone else's emotional evolution, we're reminded that society's most vulnerable and sensitive members often emerge as its most severely brutalized.

Daddy vs. Mommie vs Stepmommie:
It would be morally easier in this film if Daddy were leaving (hopelessly drunken) Mommie for someone better. Alas, that's not the case: The evil new stepmom is a territorial, over-the-hill, home-grabbing harpy who's worse (and if it's possible, even less sensitive) than the dysfunctional matriarch she's replacing. As politics and power bases shift within David's shattered family, the heterosexuals who surround him, including evil stepmom, spectacularly misdiagnose his problems. They focus instead on issues that fall within their own (limited) past experience. These include, among others, a preoccupation with the salvation of a promiscuous sister. (In a drunken, drug-enhanced stupor, she falls asleep in someone's bathtub after losing control at a wild party.) It becomes obvious that new stepmom feels more secure dealing with this than with the thornier issues raised by a gifted teenaged stepson who's gay.

Ironically, within this dismal family, the older siblings emerge as colossally apathetic narcissists. It's David who evolves into the role of caretaker for his dysfunctional mother. He also emerges as the only character who's capable of even the simplest form of nurturing, a role at which everyone who surrounds him seem spectacularly incapable. When Mommy begins hemorrhaging from a cut on her chin (the result of a drunken fall), it's David who handles the emotional and medical fallout as his siblings look on with apathetic (and judgmental) indifference.

Members of his family aren't the only ones who let David down: His ingénue teeny-bopper girlfriend is spectacularly, even voluptuously, unsupportive. After demanding (and not receiving) sexual fulfillment from David, she roars away spewing hatred, leaving his emotional landscape utterly bereft of comfort.

Into the void steps Kenny, who gets David's mother to sign over legal custody of David to his care. Self-involved Kenny, alas, isn't up to the challenge of raising a sensitive and intellectually gifted modern teenager. He lies ("Sorry, I won't ever do that [kiss you] again"), provides the drugs that David will eventually crave, and blows up into fits of jealousy over David's unexpected success at auditioning for B- and C-list movie parts. Small-spirited Kenny segués unattractively in and out of David's life throughout five subsequent years of substance abuse and addiction. Eventually, Kenny retreats completely, fading into obscurity, a Socratic role model who never rose to the

Eben Gordon

Rob Moretti

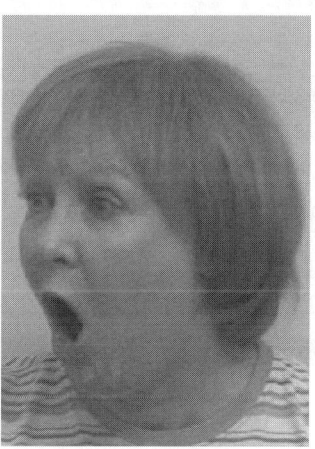

Juanita Walsh

PRODUCTION CREW:

Director of Photography: Brian Fass
Music: Ben Goldberg
Casting: Ken Schactman
Editors: Jennifer Erickson and Rob Moretti
Costume Designers: Melanie Covello and Jennifer Erickson
Makeup: Larry Fallon
Production Manager: Eric Smith

challenge of being a nurturing and supportive patriarch.

David's descent into substance abuse occurs amid the tears and teeth-gnashing of his mother's blood-soaked sheets, among which he discovers one of a series of hidden flasks. Her ingenuity for hiding her crutches evokes the cunning of the alchoholics in *Days of Wine & Roses*.) David's descent into five years of substance abuse seems fully reasonable when the viewer is confronted with the fact that nobody in his proximity seemed able to do anything except contribute to the downward spiral.

The conclusion to this tragedy of almost Greek dimensions is handled with a deft and light touch. David comes back from the brink in a way that's recited through adroit acting, adroit use of film-as-confessional, and adroit editing. What's amazing to this writer is the fact that this savvy film was produced at all--lesser mortals would have caved in to the despair. But in this case, not only did the protagonist survive, he even managed to produce this insightful and laudable film as part of the therapeutic process.

WHAT THE CRITICS SAID:

"*Crutch* does succeed in creating an intimacy with the audience. This story is so personal that you can't help but feel like a voyeur trapped in the small houses and apartments where most of the action takes place. When mom splits open her chin in a drunken stupor and blood spreads everywhere as David helps her down the stairs, you almost want to wipe the blood off your own hands."

Don Willmott

"Mr. Moretti, who wrote and directed this self-conscious but nicely structured drama, has made it very clear that David is his alter ego and that these things really happened to him. Moviegoers could probably guess that."

Anita Gates *The New York Times*

CAST OF CHARACTERS

Robert Bray (Michael); James Earley (Jack); Frankie Faison (Jerry); Eben Gordon (David); Jennifer Katz (Maryann); Tim Loftus (Zack); Rob Moretti (Kenny); Sylvia Norman (Linda); Laura O'Reilly (Lisa); Juanita Walsh (Katie); Jennifer Laine Williams (Julia)

Gypsy 83

Directed by Todd Stephens.
Written by Tim Kaltenecker and Todd Stephens.
Produced by Karen Jaroneski, Todd Stephens,
and Judith Zarin.
Released by Small Planet Pictures
and Velvet Films in association
with Luna Pictures and Staccato Films.
www.gypsy83.com
Genre: Drama
Runtime: 94 Minutes

PLOT SYNOPSIS:
Two young misfits, as played by Sara Rue and Kett Turton (portraying a gay teenager), set out for New York to attend "The Night of the 1,000 Stevies," an annual bash attracting Stevie Nicks impersonators and fans. Along the way to their horizon, they encounter various difficulties and road blocks, such as menacing frat boys. Expect run-ins and various encounters, including one with a handsome young Amish boy.

This is a tale of two young misfits, who decide to flee Ohio and pursue their dreams in New York. Sara Rue, who brilliantly portrayed Gypsy, deserves to be cast in other films. She plays an aspiring singer and songwriter working at a temp job in a drive-through photo shop. As one reviewer accurately noted, Rue plays Gypsy with "just the right combination of sweetness, sexuality, and sass." Her best friend, who shares many of her musical ambitions, is Clive. Actor Kett Turton played this gay teenager.

Kett Turton and Paulo Costanzo

Together they strike out to New York to participate in something called "The Night of 1,000 Stevies," a competition at a nightclub. This is a Stevie Nicks lookalike competition and both of the teenagers worship Stevie Nicks.

En route to their dreams, clouds get in their way. Surely this film has one of the most colorful casts of supporting players in many a year, including Polly Pearl (Stephanie McVay), White Trash Mommy (Nancy Arons), and Chi Chi Valenti (Vera Beren). Even Karen Black gets in on the action as Bambi LeBleau (don't you love that name?), playing an over-the-hill roadhouse chanteuse and karaoke hostess.

Oh, and lest we forget, the entire film is presented by director/writer Todd Stephens in the bizarre clothing of a Goth cult. And, surely, no woman in America wears her large Goth clothing with more style and daring than the Junoesque Sara Rue. If there's somebody still living in the boonies who doesn't know what Goth dress is, it is worn by young people who dress up like embalmers at a Victorian funeral parlor and who paint their faces with heavy amounts of black mascara.

Kett Turton

Sara Rue

Anson Scoville

<table>
</table>

PRODUCTION CREW:

Director of Photography: Gina Degirolamo
Executive Producers: Michael Wolfson
Music: Marty Beller
Editor: Annette Davey
Production Designer: Nancy Arons
Costume Designer: Kitty Boots

CAST OF CHARACTERS

Sara Rue (Gypsy); Kett Turton (Clive); Karen Black (Bambi LeBleau); John Doe (Ray); Carolyn Baumer (Lois); Anson Scoville (Zachariah); Paulo Constanzo (Troy); Stephanie McVay (Polly Pearl); Nancy Arons (White Trash Mommy); Vera Beren (Chi Chi Valenti)

WHAT THE CRITICS SAID:

"Leaving their home in Sandusky, Ohio, to travel in a '78 Trans Am to 'The Night of 1,000 Stevies' talent competition in Manhattan, Stevie Nicks wannabe Gypsy (Sara Rue) and her Goth pal, Clive (Kett Turton), who calls himself Robert Smith, cavort in cemeteries along the way and encounter a washed-up lounge singer. Clive gives up his virginity to a deeply closeted frat boy (Paulo Costanzo) in the same public restroom where Gypsy gets it on with a hunky Amish hitchhiker (Anson Scoville)."

Lou Lumenick *New York Post*

"A teenage road movie dressed in Goth clothing, Todd Stephens' follow-up to his acclaimed gay-themed drama *Edge of Seventeen* is mainly notable for the talents of its star, Sara Rue, whose ABC sitcom, *Less Than Perfect*, no doubt facilitated this long-delayed release. Playing a 25-year-old, overweight, Goth-styled, Stevie Nicks fanatic named Gypsy, Rue demonstrates a vivid warmth and appeal that demonstrates a bright career."

Frank Scheck *The Hollywood Reporter*

"The heroine of Mr. Stephen's film is Gypsy Vale, a large woman of 25 who wears her Goth uniform to work at the Foto Hut in a shopping mall in Sandusky, Ohio. She lives with her father, Ray, a lovable loser who once had rock star ambitions but now sells guitars for a living. But Gypsy dreams of going to New York, following in the fleet footsteps of her mother, who abandoned her family to pursue her rock star dreams."

Dave Kehr *The New York Times*

"Films like this have a way of finding their own devoted fan base, and *Gypsy 83* deserves to be discovered not only by Goth and gay crowds, but by anyone who runs screaming from all things average. Such rebel spirits should enjoy following Clive and Gypsy's road trip as they encounter a wayward Amish hunk, a washed-up lounge singer, and a corruptible frat boy en route to New York. Like *Edge*, *Gypsy 83* captures the genuine mix of achievement and disappointment that marks the formative years."

Peter Debruge *Premier*

"Several years ago, Todd Stephens wrote an affecting semi-autobiographical script for *Edge of Seventeen*, in which a high school youth struggles to accept his homosexuality. Stephens set his story in his native Sandusky, Ohio, which is also where his new film, the tender *Gypsy 83*, begins. Once again, Stephens, in his directorial debut, plays affectionate humor against the raw pain that can be the price of being different."

Kevin Thomas *Los Angeles Times*

A Home at the End of the World

Written by Michael Cunningham
(novel and screenplay).
Directed by Michael Mayer.
Released by Warner Independent Pictures.
www.warnerbros.com
Genre: Drama, Romance
Runtime: 120 minutes

PLOT SYNOPSIS:
Sexy straight star Colin Farrell plays gay in a film about another gay guy, a woman, and a baby. Expect sex, drugs, and rock 'n roll but no Farrell frontal nude.

Colin Farrell Robin Wright Penn, and Dallas Roberts

Adapted by Michael Cunningham (*The Hours*) from his 1990 novel, this film was directed by one of the year's most promising newcomers, stage director Michael Mayer. It was the romantic *ménage à trois* of 2004, but with a definite gay twist, carrying an R rating for its strong drug content, sexuality, nudity, language, and a disturbing accident. But what generated headlines around the world was a frontal nude shot of Colin that was removed from the final release, although seen by preview audiences. See box, "Colin Farrell: The Unkindest Cut."

In the film, the real-life, headline-making wild Irish boy, Colin, plays an orphan Bobby Morrow in a story that moves from 1967 to the 1980s era of "the plague." Orphaned as a teenager, Bobby comes to live with his friend Jonathan, as played by Dallas Roberts. When the two boys are caught smoking pot by Mom, as interpreted by the always brilliant Sissy Spacek, she joins them to enjoy a little weed herself. Growing up with Jonathan, Bobby is the sweetest boy who ever lived. Gay Jonathan falls for his bedmate, and sexual experimentation follows.

As the years go by, Jonathan has left for New York City, where he leads an openly gay life. Eventually Bobby follows him there from Cleveland, finding Jonathan living with an

Colin Farrell: The Unkindest Cut

Irish heartthrob's Colin Farrell's full frontal movie scene was cut from the final release of *A Home at the End of the World*. The "size of his manhood"--read that *huge*--stunned viewers at test run screenings. "He was just too big for the screen," the director said. "It was just too distracting."

Many potential viewers, especially gay men, threatened to boycott the film because the penis shot was cut. (Incidentally, foreskin lovers, Colin's penis might have been cut from the film, but, like many an Irish lad, it's uncut in real life).

The *Phone Booth* hunk had no trouble disrobing. Colin claimed that he's very casual about stripping down for the full monty.

Actually, in spite of the headlines to the contrary, *A Home at the End of the World* was not Colin's first foray in nudity. His naked scenes in Joel Schumacher's *Tigerland* earned him appreciative gay audiences back in 2000. At the time Colin--falsely and far too modestly--claimed that "My bits looked the size of a cashew nut!"

We don't know what size of a cashew nut Colin is used to eating, but the size of his penis led to such headlines in the *San Francisco Chronicle* as WHEN A PENIS IS TOO BIG TO SEE.

"The dimensions of Colin's offending member overexcited the women and the men looked really uncomfortable," one critic said. "No doubt it was a case of penis envy."

Veteran movie critic Roger Ebert claimed that the director was correct in this well-publicized decision to leave out Colin's full frontal. "The movie is not about the size or function of Bobby's penis," Ebert wrote, "but about its friend-liness."

Colin, speaking about his own "circumcision" in the film, said, "The problem is that they (a reference to newspaper editors) are just going, 'Oh, my God, Colin Farrell's cock. Shit! So, let's write about that. Was it too big? Was it too small? Was it too wide? Was it too skinny? Was it an innie or an outtie. I know the reason that it was cut out was that it just wasn't right. If anything, it's a beautiful, gentle moment and a fucking large cock with huge balls is just fuck-ing jarring!"

eccentric hatmaker roommate, Clare, as played luminously by Robin Wright Penn. In no time at all, the trio has created a makeshift family.

Clare is really a fag hag and falls for Jonathan's boyhood friend. Eventually they move to Woodstock, New York, presumably the end of the world, at least in the view of Cunningham. Clare manages to seduce Bobby after he confesses that he's a virgin. A daughter is the result of their liaison.

The nontraditional family as depicted in the film was attacked by the religious right but was all about love. We won't spoil the ending by telling you which character, Jonathan or Clare, the placid Bobby chooses at the end of the film. But we're left with the distinct impression that his choice was based not just on his sexual pleasure, but on which friend, Clare or Jonathan, needed him the most.

Colin, playing an innocent with a bad haircut, is miscast, or maybe his off-screen bad boy image is too strong in our minds. The other actors outshine Colin, especially scene-stealing Spacek as the mother. Both Roberts, a newcomer, and Robin Wright Penn add depth and meaning to the somewhat sappy drama.

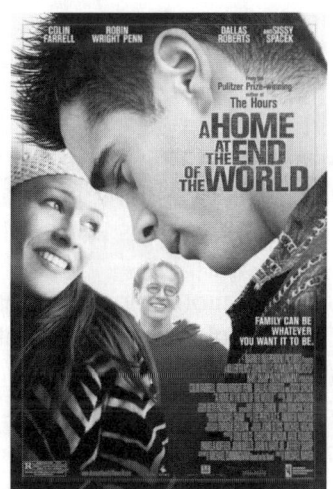

Robin Wright Penn

Colin Farrell

Sissy Spacek

WHAT THE CRITICS SAID:

"By the time Bobby is a teenager (played by a sensitive young actor named Erik Smith), he has pretty much lost his original family. He is welcomed into the home of Jonathan Glover (Harris Allan), a gawky, gangly schoolmate, whose mother, Alice (Sissy Spacek), comes to regard Bobby as a second son. In the movie's best scene, he introduces her to the music of Laura Nyro and to marijuana, which makes Jonathan understandably uncomfortable. Later, in 1982, Bobby, who has been living with Alice and her husband in Cleveland, follows Jonathan (now played by Dallas Roberts) to New York and becomes the hypotenuse in a romantic triangle that also includes their roommate, a free-spirited, somewhat older woman named Clare (Robin Wright Penn).

Families, the movie suggests, can be destroyed by accident and made by a combination of good luck and good will. It has much gentle wisdom to offer about the fragility and the durability of human connections and about the acceptance of death that is necessary for a full appreciation of life."

A.O. Scott *The New York Times*

"While the novel explores the minutiae that threaten the delicate balance of this bizarre love triangle, the film leaves us wondering what Bobby's friends see in him."

Jorge Morales *The Village Voice*

"The movie exists outside our expectations for such stories. Nothing about it is conventional. The three-member household is puzzling not only to us, but to its members. We expect conflict, resolution, an ending happy or sad, but what we get is mostly life, muddling through. Some days are good and other days are bad."

Rogert Ebert

"Hang on to your hats everyone. Clasp your headgear and get the tightest grip possible on your millinery. Sexy star Colin Farrell plays gay! Alpha-hetero hellraiser Colin daringly plays someone of the homosexual persuasion and makes a frowningly serious thespian journey into the heart of the invert universe. I don't think he could look more gay than in those photos as *Alexander the Great*, but there you go."

Peter Bradshaw *The Guardian*

WHAT THE CRITICS SAID (CONT'D):

"It might take a bit to adjust to wild Irish boyo Colin Farrell playing Bobby Morrow, a twentysomething virgin who moves from Cleveland to New York to live with his gay friend Jonathan (newcomer Dallas Roberts is a genuine find) and Clare (a vivid Robin Wright Penn), the wiggy bohemian hatmaker Jonathan is shacked up with. But adjust you will, since Farrell's astutely judged portrayal -- he finds the crucial streak of manipulation in Bobby's sweetness -- is a career highlight. Stage director Michael Mayer (Side Man) makes a striking debut in film, and his skill with the actors is often breathtaking. Sissy Spacek triumphs in the supporting role of Jonathan's suburban mother. In a childhood flashback, she discovers the boys smoking grass and listening to Laura Nyro's lush "Desiree" and joins them as if discovering a new world. Spacek's revelatory performance (hello, Oscar) is typical of the film's eye for detail as Bobby, Jonathan and Clare make up their own definition of family. In adapting his 19TK novel to the screen, Michael Cunningham (The Hours) must condense a story that moves from 1967 to the 1980s AIDS era into a sometimes rushed ninety minutes. But how many movies these days leave you wanting more? The funny and heartfelt Home is a small treasure. "

Peter Travers *Rolling Stone*

CAST OF CHARACTERS

Andrew Chalmers (Bobby Morrow); Ryan Donowho (Carlton Morrow); Asia Vieira (Emily); Quancetia Hamilton (Dancing Party Guest); Jeff J.J. Authors (Frank); Lisa Merchant (Frank's Date), Ron Lea (Burt Morrow); Erik Smith (Bobby Morrow 1974); Harris Allan (Jonathan Glover 1974); Matt Frewer (Ned Glover); Sissy Spacek (Alice Glover); Colin Farrell (Bobby Morrow 1982); Dallas Roberts (Jonathan Glover 1982); Robin Wright Penn(Clare); Shawn Roberts (Club Boy)

PRODUCTION CREW:

Director of Photography:	Enrique Chediak
Art Direction:	Edward Bonutto
Music:	Duncan Sheik
Casting:	Jim Carnahan and Claire Simon
Editor:	Andrew Marcus and Lee Percy
Set Decoration:	Malcolm Byard, Linette Forbes Shorr, and Mark Steel

Junked

Written and Directed by Lance Lane.
Produced by Lance Lane.
Released by Harley's House/Junked Productions
in association with Hollywood Independents.
www.hollywood.com/movies
Genre: Street Drama
Runtime: 86 Minutes

PLOT SYNOPSIS:
Based on a real life story, this film, adapted from an original play, describes the rough road that Switch, a former thug, faces in his attempt to go straight. He finds that fleeing from street life isn't easy. If he wants to get out alive, he has to figure out how to escape from his past – and vengeance – with himself intact.

Jordan Ladd and Thomas Jane

Inspired by actual events, this is street drama at its starkest. *Junked* is a little known film that is not everyone's cuppa, but it has its devotees. It tells the story of a former criminal, as played effectively by actor Thomas Jane, trying to go straight.

Fearing for his life, he wants to flee the street life, if that's possible at this point. Switch wants to go straight not just for himself, but for his best friend, Jimmy, played by Channing Rowe in a memorable appearance. Switch's kid sister, Nikki, is brought to the screen by Jordan Ladd in a completely convincing performance as a junkie and prostitute. Given this premise, the film sets out to explore how difficult it is for Switch to go straight. Vengeance is waiting to engulf him. The score by Kurt Weill helps a lot. The depiction of criminal low-lifes who inhabit the streets is stark and realistic, so much so that one reviewer called the film "almost unwatchable."

The picture clearly belongs to Thomas Jane, a promising actor best known for his starring roles *in The Punisher* and *Dreamcatcher.* In *Junked*, he plays the role of a bisexual hustler, and does it with a certain style.

Junked first saw the light as a play but it has been successfully adapted to the screen. The movie was a long time in being filmed. Budget considerations were no doubt responsible. Actual filming began in 1998 with the completion date not coming until 2004.

Naturally, you expect drug abuse and strong language. "Of course," we heard one movie-goer comment, "Why else would we be here?"

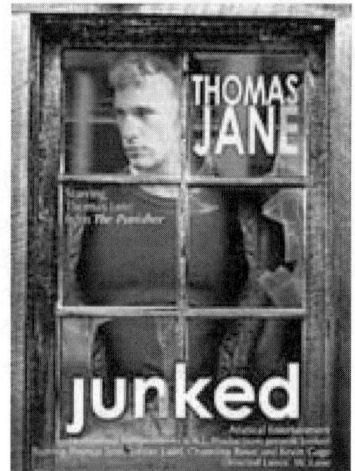

Jordan Ladd   Thomas Jane

WHAT THE CRITICS SAID:

"Unfortunately Switch's past doesn't want to be forgotten, and when vengeance comes knocking at his door, he must revert to his old ways if he wants to get out alive."

Jason Buchanan *All Movie Guide*

"What keeps the experience from being painful – but cannot elevate it above the level of an unpleasant curiosity – is the presence of Thomas Jane, an engaging actor who has made a name for himself in major features (*The Sweetest Thing*, for one). He plays Switch, a bisexual hustler who is trying to raise money to get a friend, Jimmy, out of town. Jimmy, who is going out with Switch's sister, killed someone the night before. The sister, Nikki, a junkie and a prostitute, is played by Jordan Lane, who has a nice, sad honesty as an actress. Either that, or she's pretty enough to make anyone think so."

Mick LaSalle *San Francisco Chronicle*

CAST OF CHARACTERS

Kevin Cage (Crow); Thomas Jane (Switch);
Jordan Ladd (Nikki); Channing Rowe (Jimmy)

PRODUCTION CREW:

Executive Producer: Lance Lane
Producer: Marion Lane
Film Editor   Jim Monroe

Kinsey

Written and Directed by Bill Condon.
Produced by Gail Mutrux.
Released by Fox Searchlight Pictures
in association with Qwerty Films.
A NI European Film Produktions/American
Zoetrope/Pretty Pictures Production.
www.fox-searchlight.com/press.
Genre: Biography
Runtime: 118 Minutes

PLOT SYNOPSIS:
*Academy Award winner Bill Condon (***Gods and Monsters***) turns the microscope on Alfred Kinsey in a portrait of a man driven to uncover the most private sexual secrets of a nation. What begins for Kinsey as a scientific endeavor soon takes on an intensely personal relevance, ultimately becoming an unexpected journey into the mystery of human behavior.*

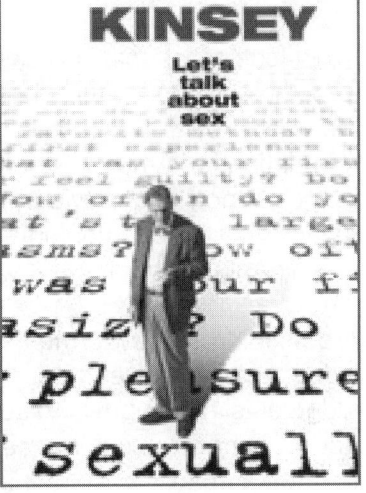

Liam Neeson

Professor Kinsey is a remarkable man in this film. He's smart enough to launch a sexual revolution, smart enough to get it funded by nothing less than the (very uptight at the time) Rockefeller Foundation, and smart enough to avoid unpleasant accusations of Communist leanings from the (then dauntingly powerful) McCarthyites. He's even smart enough to take things gracefully in stride when the sexual energies of his good-looking male research assistant are unleashed first upon Kinsey himself (we learn as the film unfolds that Kinsey is part of the 48% of the American population that his famous study defines as bisexual), and then upon his wife, a role that's played with aplomb by Laura Linney. So it's early established that the Kinseys both swing and switch-hit, and it's later hinted that the members of their research team probably go considerably farther. But like lots of the sexual gambits of the late 40s and 50s, it's all very subtle and--historically speaking--never seemed to get so out of hand that it was actually exposed within the era's press.

Even though it might have been nonstandard, the Kinsey's marital bliss didn't come without some bumps and grinds along the way. Mrs. Kinsey, it's revealed, had a thick-walled and particularly robust hymen that made penetration from donkey-dong Kinsey (we learn that he has a prodigious willie during a scene at her gynecologist's office) virtually impossible. Early in the film, thanks to an enlightened surgeon, Venus's barrier is surgically and painlessly cut asunder, coitus is fulfilled with panache by the good doctor himself, and the now happily fornicating couple is baptized in the fire of their conviction that a fulfilling sex life is the inevitable result of an enlightened program of sex education.

The drama of *Kinsey*, and the heroism of the film's namesake, derives from the conflict at the time between the yearning of the American populace to correspond to standards of sexual "normalcy" during an era when no one had a clue as to what "sexual normalcy" meant. The identification of prevalent standards of sexual behavior was virtually impossible during an era when even the most prestigious academics had virtually no scientific data about the sexual behavior of the "average" American person.

Kinsey, in an efficient and carefully edited presentation that leaves out a lot of dry and boring statistics, shows the evolution of the Kinseynian method. Kinsey, a prophet in the wilderness, uses his status as a celebrated authority on the mating habits of the gall wasp to launch a whole new way of looking and talking about sex among humans. Hard on his heels, within a decade or two, but presumably nurtured by some of the conclusions expressed in his report, would come the gyrating pelvis of Elvis Presley, the accentuated boobs of Jayne Mansfield, the coy and coquettish "delayed fuck" presentation of Rock Hudson and Doris Day's *Pillow Talk*, and the counter-culture sexual flagrancy of The Woodstock generation and The Doors. And later, gay lib.

Kinsey, as eloquently and alluringly played by Liam Neeson (was the real Kinsey as good-looking as that?) rocks and rolls confidently through the evolution of his sexual hypotheses. With an endearing kind of open-handedness, he bumbles and blunders his way through the compilation of statistical information that will, eventually, rock the foundations of America's self-image. "Do you masturbate?" even when queried within the cocoon of a movie set and replayed on DVD, still elicits some of the same red-faced "aw shucks" apologies that we might have experienced in sex-ed classes back in junior high school.

A crusading Kinsey, armed with notepads and plenty of sharpened pencils, repeatedly lectures his survey-takers against the dangers of loading their questions with value judgments. He submits to such a questionnaire himself, admitting the he's between 30 and 40% homosexual himself, and then passionately kisses his male research assistant, presumably for personal fulfillment as much as for an extension of his research.

And on a hot Saturday night when he's dressed in a way that's particularly academic, rumpled, and tweedy, he even barges--"purely for research purposes"--into a crowded gay bar to survey the denizens of the night. He's greeted with a mixture of irony, apathy, and eventually, respect, as some of the patrons allow themselves to be surveyed under the flattering laser-beams of his research team. More poignantly, and with oceans of grace (could we mortals behave as elegantly?), he even triumphs in the "reconciliation of the child with the man" department by lovingly and intelligently interviewing his impossibly judgmental and punitive father (as played by John Lithgow, whose roles are usually a lot more likable) about his own sexual identity, awakening some interesting sleeping dragons as part of the process.

With the benefit of historical hindsight, anyone who makes the effort to see this film probably already defines him or herself as both politically correct and at least to some degree, sexually enlightened. But some scenes within the film resonate with the pain of the postwar era's sexual repression and its aftereffects. The film culminates with the thanks expressed to Kinsey by one of society's then-deviates, a kindly looking, blue-eyed Anglo-Saxon grandmother who might have inspired a Norman Rockwell version of a poster girl for the Religious Right.   It turns out that Grannie is a lesbian, deeply in love with another woman. Prior to the publication of Kinsey's report, she was mired in guilt and corrosive loneliness, with a predilection toward alchoholism. Thanks to the revelations of The Report, she's seen the Light, maintains a loving same-sex relationship with her unnamed beloved, abandoned all forms of substance abuse, and rejected the compulsion to conform to any conception of "normalcy." Kissing Kinsey's hand, as would a member of the Catholic faithful to their Pope, she blesses him, articulating the debt all of us modern-day fags and dykes owe to Professor Kinsey and his workaholic eccentricities. The role of the grandmotherly "final interview subject," incidentally, is movingly played by Lynn Redgrave.

| Laura Linney | Liam Neeson | Peter Sarsgaard |

PRODUCTION CREW:

Director of Photography: Frederick Elmes
Executive Producers: Michael Kuhn, Francis Ford Coppola, Bobby
                         Rock, and Kirk D'Amico
Music: Carter Burwell
Editor   Virginia Katz
Production Designer: Richard Sherman
Costume Designer: Bruce Finlayson

WHAT THE CRITICS SAID:

"*Kinsey* is intense, intelligent, and deepy absorbing. It is a tribute to a great man decades ahead of his time. Liam Neeson gives his usual powerful performance, and if there is a better young leading lady than Laura Linney, I don't know who she is."

Jeffrey Lyons *NBC*

"What was shocking in the 50s is still provocative today thanks to a well told story of a true sexual revolution pioneer Dr. Alfred Kinsey, beautifully acted by Liam Neeson, with Laura Linney equally strong as his wife. Bill Condon directs his own screenplay with fervor, flair, and finesse."

David Sheehan *Hollywood Close-Ups*

"Neeson plays Kinsey as a flinty, fearless, bullying obsessive crusader whose glory, as well as his mania, is that he saw human beings, including himself, as specimens in a grand design."

Owen Gleiberman *Entertainment Weekly*

"*Kinsey* toys with the very nature of sex, not to mention love, its occassional and often troublesome by-product."

Bruce Handy *Vanity Fair*

"Kinsey is an intelligent, moving and surprisingly funny look at an unlikely revolution."

Michael Wilmington *Chicago Tribune*

CAST OF CHARACTERS

Liam Neeson (Alfred Kinsey); Laura Linney (Clara McMillen); Chris O'Donnell (Wardell Pomeroy); Peter Sarsgaard (Clyde Martin); Timothy Hutton (Paul Gebhard); John Lithgow (Alfred Seguine Kinsey); Tim Curry (Thurman Rice); Oliver Platt (Herman Wells); Dylan Baker (Alan Gregg); Lynn Redgrave (Final Interview Subject); Julianne Nicholson (Alice Martin); William Sadler (Kenneth Braun); John McMartin (Huntington Hartford); Veronica Cartwright (Sara Kinsey); Kathleen Chalfant (Barbara Merkle); Heather Goldenhersh (Martha Pomeroy); Dagmara Dominczyk (Agnes Gebhard); Susan Blommaert (Staff Secretary); Benjamin Walker (Kinsey at 19); Matthew Fahey (Kinsey at 14); Will Denton (Kinsey at 10); John Krasinski (Ben); Arden Myrin (Emily); Romulus Linney (Rep. B. Carroll Reece); Katharine Houghton (Mrs. Spaulding); David Harbour (Robert Kinsey); Judith J.K. Polson (Mildred Kinsey); Leigh Spofford (Anne Kinsey); Jenna Gavigan (Joan Kinsey); Luke MacFarlane (Bruce Kinsey); Mike Thurstlic (Kenneth Hand); Bill Buell (Dr. Thomas Lattimore)

The Real Alfred Kinsey

Alfred Kinsey

Liam Neeson

Production Notes Snipits

When Kinsey published his *Sexual Behavior in the Human Male* in 1948, the press compared the impact to that of the atom bomb. Soon Kinsey graced the cover of every major publication. He became the subject of cartoons, editorials, and sermons. But as the country entered the more paranoid Cold War era of the 1950s, Kinsey's follow-up study on women was seen as an attack on basic American values. The ensuing outrage and scorn caused Kinsey's benefactors to abandon him, just as his health began to deteriorate. At the same time, the jealousies and acrimony caused by Kinsey's attempt to create a private sexual utopia threatened to tear apart the research team and expose its members to unwelcome scrutiny.

Kinsey spent his last days in a vain attempt to secure funding. He died in 1956, fearing that his life's work had been a failure. In the film version, at least, it was only through his contact with a final interview subject that he glimpsed the positive effect he had. He also began to understand that the basic question of where sex ends and love begins was something that can never be completely answered by science.

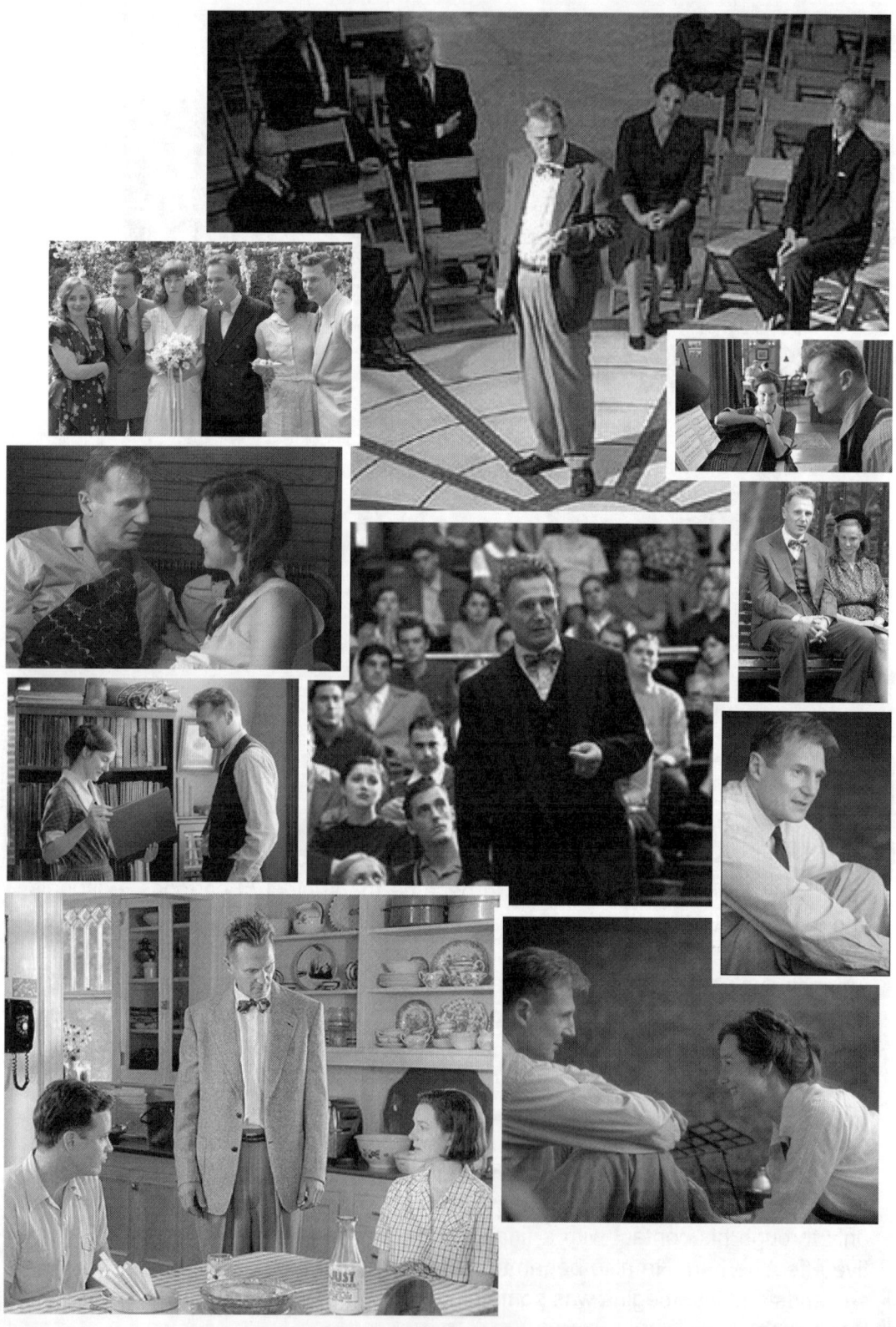

Latter Days

Written and directed by C. Jay Cox.
Produced by J. Todd Harris, Kermit Johns
and Scott Zimmerman.
Released by Funny Boy Films
in association with TLA Releasings.
www.latterdaysmovie.com
Genre: Comedy/Drama/Romance
Runtime: 107 Minutes

PLOT SYNOPSIS:
Opposites attract. In this
case Elder Aaron Davis
(Steve Sandvoss) plays a
Mormon missionary and Wes
Ramsey a slutty West
Hollywood party boy,
Christian. On a $50 bet,
Christian sets out to seduce
Davis, a latent homosexual.
Can love bloom in the
homophobic Mormon
Church? The drama and
romance hinges on that very
problem. To announce your-
self as gay in the Mormon
Church in like admitting
you're a witch in Old Salem.

Expect fireworks when a wild, gay "party ani-mal" falls for a handsome young Mormon mis-sionary. Needless to say, the Mormons are not known for promoting gay liberation.

Christian, as charmingly played by Wes Ramsey, is a hunky, 20-something, West Hollywood slut. He gets more than he bargains for when he tries to seduce 19-year-old Elder Aaron Davis, as delightfully acted by Steve Sandvoss, so boyishly handsome you'll want to abduct him.

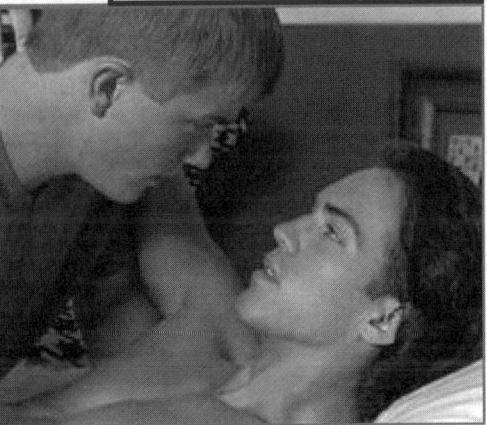

Steve Sandvoss and Wes Ramsey

Davis is a sexually confused Mormon missionary who moves into an apartment complex in gay West Hollywood.

When Christian exposes Davis's secret sexual desires, Davis rejects Christian for being shallow and empty. The encounter shatters each boy's reality, drawing the two into a passionate romance that risks destroying their lives.

Latter Days is charming, sexy, and moving, a tale that will leave you believing in the transformational power of love.

Jacqueline Bisset comes as a total and rather delightful surprise in this film. She is the tolerant owner of a restaurant where Christian works as a waiter.

This is the directorial debut of C. Jay Cox, a long way from home and his screenplay for the romantic comedy, *Sweet Home Alabama.*

The film ran into trouble in Salt Lake City where it provoked outrage among some members og the Mormon community. We weren't there, but would love to have stood in the lobby to see if any gay-bashing Mormons showed up.

For the most part, the characters, except for the gay-haters, are well conceived and sympathetic.

PRODUCTION CREW:

Director of Photography: Carl Bartels
Music: Eric Allaman
Editor: John Keitel
Production Designer: Chris Anthony Miller
Art Direction: Nanet Harty
Set Decoration: Peter Ayala
Assistant Directors: Thom Buckley, Ed Cha, Darin Fenn
Sound: Garrett Bradley, Tommy Goodwin, and Jim Ridgley

CAST OF CHARACTERS

Steve Sandvoss (Elder Aaron Davis); Wes Ramsey (Christian Markelli); Rebekah Johnson (Julie Taylor); Amber Benson (Traci Levine); Khary Payton (Andrew); Jacqueline Bisset (Lila Montagne); Joseph Gordon-Levitt (Elder Paul Ryder); Rob McElhenney (Elder Harmon); Dave Power (Elder Gilford); Erik Palladino (Keith Griffin); Mark Kay Place (Sister Gladys Davis); Jim Ortlieb (Brother Farron Davis); Linda Pine (Susan Davis); Bob Gray (Susan's Husband); Judith Fraser (Noreen)

Wes Ramsey

Steve Sandvoss

Joseph Gordon Levitt

WHAT THE CRITICS SAID:

"The movie, written and directed by C. Jay Cox, mixes a bright young cast with canny, sparkling veterans like Jacqueline Bisset and Mary Kay Place. And the film is an odd mix itself, of contemporary sexual realism and unabashed romantic fantasy. If "Days" works, it's mostly on a sheer fantasy level."

Michael Wilmington *Chicago Tribune*

"We can't tell you what happens next because we're not going to ruin this romantic drama for you, but C. Jay Cox is a Hollywood screenwriter with all that entails. His work on *Sweet Home Alabama* which included a great gay character, brought kudos, but this is clearly his project of love. The incredibly handsome and charismatic Sandvoss, in his debut film, gives us fierce non-verbal emotion that few actors can match – watch this boy's career. All of the acting is first-rate, including Amber Benson and Christian's co-worker, Mary Kay Place as Aaron's stern mother and Jacqueline Bisset as Christian's restaurant boss who harbors her own secrets. It's a grand gay screen romance with large-scale emotions that belongs in everyone's collections."

Scott Cranin *International Film Festival*

"Christian, played by the former soap opera star Wes Ramsey, is that stock figure of gay drama, the hopelessly handsome party boy whose life is devoted to casual sex. A waiter in a Los Angeles restaurant owned and operated by the radiantly maternal Lila (the always welcome Jacqueline Bisset), Christian accepts a $50 wager from his co-workers that he will be able to seduce Aaron (Steve Sandvoss), an apparently straight Mormon missionary who has moved into an apartment opposite his. Following one of Hollywood's favorite clichés, what begins as a cynical bet develops into a deep romance. After some initial resistance, Aaron surrenders to Christian's charms, discovering his homosexuality in the process. At the same time Christian discovers, in Aaron's sincerity and innocence, the deeper values that have been missing from his own life."

Dave Kehr *New York Times*

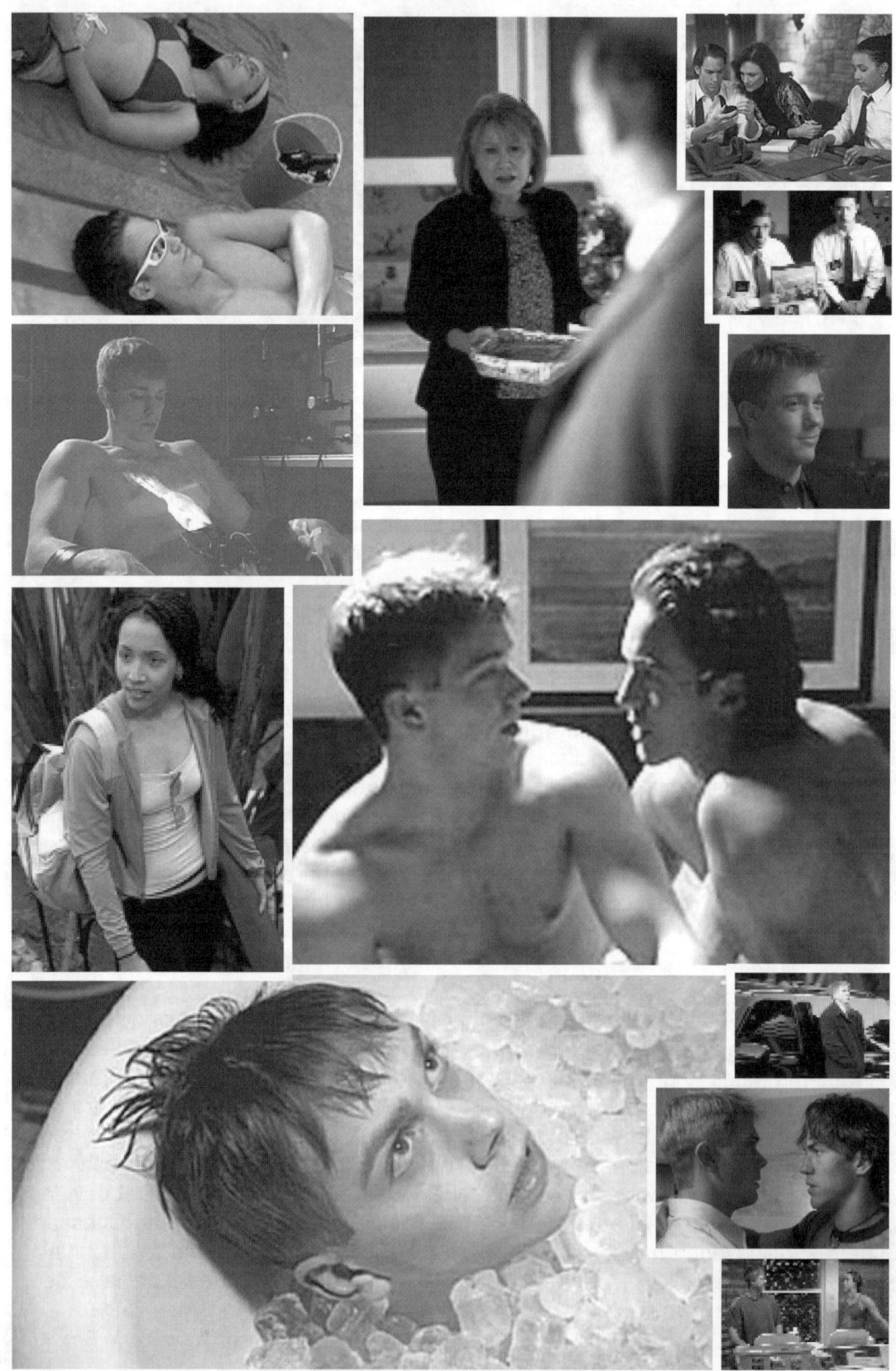

Merci Docteur Rey

Written and directed by Andrew Litvack.
Produced by Ismail Merchant.
Released by Eat Your Soup Productions
in association with Here! Films.
www.mercidocteurrey.com
Genre: Comedy
Runtime: 91 Minutes

PLOT SYNOPSIS:
In this French farce, a 23-year-old gay son of an opera diva answers anonymous personal ads and, not by design, witnesses the murder of his own father while hiding in a bedroom closet. All the characters contrive to foil the subsequent police investigation.

Stanislas Merhar and Jane Birkin

The latest Merchant and Ivory film is unlike any of their other films you've seen so far. Actually, it is a showcase for first-time writer and director Andrew Litvack.

Playing an opera diva, Dianne Wiest is the mother of a sexually confused son, as interpreted by Stanislas Merhar. In Paris, he spends his day calling hustlers who take out classified ads. Evoking *Dressed to Kill*, Thomas witnesses one of the participants in a pre-planned tryst murdered before his eyes.

It turns out that Thomas has unwittingly witnessed his own father's murder. Up to then, his mother has told him that his father was dead. He leaves home in search of the killer.

Hiding out for a good part of the movie, Stanislas, playing Thomas, is aided by his friend, Jane Birkin, appearing as Pénélope, a neurotic actress. Jerry Hall and Vanessa Redgrave, perhaps not known to very young audiences, appear in cameos.
They provide evidence that time, indeed, is marching on. We admire Litvack for providing work of these grande dames, including Bulle Ogier. Expect a delirious finish to all this cockamamie plot, as Litvack rushes with panache to the finish line.

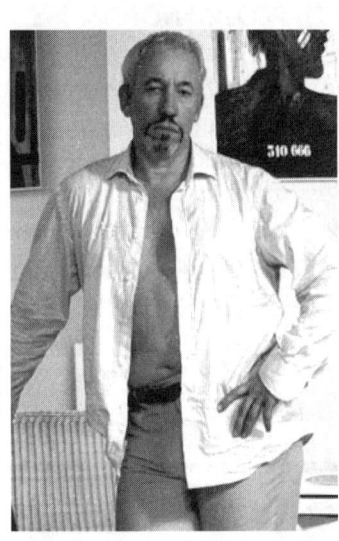

Simon Callow

Jane Birkin

Dianne Wiest

PRODUCTION CREW:

Director of Photography: Laurent Machuel
Music: Geoff Alexander
Editor: Giles Gardner
Production Management: Sylvain Monod
Assistant Director: Patrick Roques

CAST OF CHARACTERS

Dianne Wiest (Elizabeth Beaumont); Jane Birkin (Pénélope); Stanislas Merhar (Thomas Beaumont); Bulle Ogier (Claude Sabrié); Karim Salah (Murderer); Didier Flamand (Detective); Roschdy Zem (Taxi Driver); Nathalie Richard (Radio Interviewer); Dan Herzberg (Rollerboy); Jerry Hall (Sybil); Simon Callow (Bob); Vanessa Redgrave (Herself); Vernon Dobtcheff (François)

WHAT THE CRITICS SAID:

"The latest Merchant & Ivory offering, by first-time writer-director Andrew Litvack, is an uneasy amalgam of farce and prestige, as if Almodóvar's "Woman on the Verge of a Nervous Breakdown" had been produced by, well, Merchant & Ivory. Moviegoers may be lured in by the comedic promise of seeing Dianne Wiest as an opera diva (her other diva turn, in "Bullets over Broadway," deservedly netted her an Oscar)…"

Joe Mader *Mill Valley Film Festival*

"If anything, in this 'you'll love it or hate it' movie, homosexuality is just used as an 'extended metaphor' for a string of 'hang-ups.' However, both Litvack and Birkin agree that the audience's response is 'something else' at gay and lesbian film fests. 'On one occasion the laughter was so uproarious that we couldn't hear the lines. I'm glad James Ivory was in the room to witness it because I couldn't believe it myself!'"

Georgia Oliver *Paris Voice*

"Dianne Wiest plays a prima donna proffering an indifference to the world as opaque as the Sophia Loren sunglasses she wears. Her son Thomas, confined to their huge Paris pad, can only gratify himself by sneaking out to meet rent boys while mother's preoccupied with her latest whine fit."

David Blaylock *Village Voice*

"'Curb your Narcissism.' And 'Divas make me Puke.' Those are among the out-landish catch phrases bandied by the garrulous hothouse creatures flitting through the farcical mystery, "Merci Docteur Rey." The movie, written and directed by Andrew Litvack, a protégé of Ismail Merchant and James Ivory, strains to be the ne plus ultra of arch, hyper-sophisticated fun…"

Stephen Holden *New York Times*

"*Merci Docteur Rey* offers an extremely slender – yet most beguiling – excuse for showcasing a clutch of celebrated actresses of a certain age. The plot is unabashedly implausible, but it expresses first-time writer-director Andrew Litvack's giddy, amused sense of life's absurdities. An elegant Merchant Ivory Production, it is too slight and perhaps too precious. But it will be a witty pleasure for admirers of its grande dames: Dianne Wiest, Jane Birkin and Bulle Ogier, with an appearance by Vanessa Redgrave as herself."

Kevin Thomas *Los Angeles Times*

My Mother Likes Women

(A mi madre le gustan las mujeres)

Written and directed by Daniela Fejerman
and Inés París.
Released by Norador Productions.
www.mymotherlikeswomen.com
Genre: Comedy
Runtime: 93 Minutes
Spanish with English Subtitles

PLOT SYNOPSIS:
Sofia introduces her three adult daughters to her new lover, who is their age and happens to be a woman. The sisters, each mired in their respective age-appropriate crises, first try to demolish, and then succeed at resurrecting the love affair, each hammering out their life issues and broadening, as part of the process, their definition of "family."

Within the first few minutes of this film, we're introduced to Sofia (Mamma as played by one of the most famous sitcom actresses in Spain, the intensely likable Rosa María Sardà), who happens to be a celebrated concert pianist and about as hip as they come. Gathering her clan to-gether, she breathlessly

Silvia Abascal, Maria Pujalte, and Leonor Watling

announces that she's in love. Before her three daughters can even ask whether the newcomer is good in the sack, or worthy of her, the doorbell rings. The newest usurp-er to home and hearth is a statuesque (female) brunette.

The rest of the film involves how the clan copes, as they each hammer their way through their primal fear of confronting the sexuality of a parent. Each of the three con-siders herself as too liberal, and too well-educated, to outwardly reject their mother's proclivities. Reasonably, one of the sisters says to the others, "No one ever died of having a lesbian mother." But, then, like the three implacable witches of *Hamlet*, they collectively wave their arms, grieve, rage, and scheme, each with differing degrees of ruthlessness. Adding to their conviction to end the relationship is the news that Mamma has spent all her savings on paying off some of her new lover's debts.

The youngest, and perhaps the least neurotic of the three sisters, is Sol (Silvia

95

Abascal), a blissfully self-involved, pink-haired and exhibitionistic groupie who struts her stuff on stage every weekend with a punk-rock band. Her means of coping with her mother's news involves writing and performing a (tasteless and rather lewd but in a punk-rock way, sort of engaging) musical ode to her mother's taste for women, an *oeuvre* that she performs in front of hundreds of witnesses in a spectacularly insensitive delivery that slices deep.

The oldest sister Jimena (María Pujalte) is a hard-edged, unhappily married suburbanite with young son and an uptight and judgmental hubby whom she later divorces. It is she who urges her siblings to entrap her mother's new lover (Eliska) into a sexually compromising situation that will so enrage their mother as to precipitate the end of the affair. ("If I can get into Eliska's panties, then Mom will come to her senses and dump her.") Sol, the most sexually toughened of the lot, agrees to do the dirty deed. But her seduction is sabotaged when sister number two, Elvira (Leonor Watling), undermines the crude scheme in a fit of guilt and remorse. Later, it is the much deeper bond, which carries just a whiff of lesbian attraction with it) between biological daughter Elvira and surrogate daughter and lover Eliska that plays an important part of the plot line and the eventual reconciliation of all parties.

Elvira is played by Leonor Watling, an Anglo-Spanish brunette who has appeared in other films by Pedro Almodóvar, emerges as the star of this tale. Spectacularly neurotic, she's constantly on the verge of a nervous breakdown in a style that some film critics have referred to as "Almodóvarian." She's "underemployed" as an editor in a struggling publishing house, squandering her time and talent on boring production-related tasks. Confronted with the news of her mother's sexuality, and terrified that she might be a dyke-in-waiting, she vents her confusion in front of witnesses who include her lecherous therapist, her dismissive and manipulative boss, and most destructively of all, the man of her dreams, a respected author as played by the handsome and charming Chisco Amado.

Assuming, perhaps narcissistically, that her mother's lesbianism has something to do with her, she manages--thanks to the engaging humor of the actress who plays her--to remain adorable despite behavior and assumptions that in the hands of a lesser artist, would be boring and obnoxious.

Crucial to Elvira's acceptance of the situation, and her eventual adoption of Eliska as a genuine friend, are the ministrations of her father, as played by Xabier Elorriaga. A reclusive academic who divorced her mother many years previously, he's a role model for a well-adjusted older guy who is a rock for Elvira, the most vulnerable of his three daughters, to lean on. He takes the news of his ex-wife's lesbianism with grace, reading to Elvira from the love poems of Sappho when she insists on a reaction from him. His confidence and calm transform him into the most attractive male in the film. Particularly poignant is a scene where he bonds

Leonor Watling and Eliska Sirova

96

with his woman-child middle daughter over dialogue beside and within a swimming pool. The film's funniest line? When Mamma introduces her three daughters to her new lover, she explains with a touch of embarrassment that their names (Elvira, Sol, and Jimena) were selected by their father, "an intellectual," because they represented the names of the women in the life of El Cid. It's all very Iberian hip, and all very sexually sophisticated stuff, delivered at a pace that's appealingly fast.

Leonor Watling

Rosa María Sardà and Eliska Sirova

PRODUCTION CREW:

Director of Photography: David Omedes
Music: Juan Bardem and Andy Chango
Makeup: Alma Casal and Mariló Osuna
Sound Department: José Vinader and David Álvarez

WHAT THE CRITICS SAID:

"Elvira, who at times seems perfect for Renée Zellweger to play in an American remake (which wouldn't be a bad idea), is problematic: Too dysfunctional to survive and too unstable for people around her to tolerate. Even in comedy there are limits."

Steven Warren *TWN*

"Leonor Watling's pratfalls and overcaffeinated shrieking seem to be making up for having spent most of Pedro Almovódar's *Talk to Her* in a coma."

Wesley Morris *The Boston Globe*

"Although *My Mother Likes Women* was not directed by Pedro Almovódar, 'This is an Almovódarian erotic romp that suggests that in contemporary Spain, Mr. Almodóvar is a determining force in his country's loosening sexual attitudes.'"

Stephen Holden *The New York Times*

"Lightness of touch, vibrant performances and a sharp script are the hallmarks of the delightful femme comedy *My Mother Likes Women*, debut pic from writer-directors Inés París and Daniela Fejerman. Despite its misleadingly cheesy title and over-hasty wrap-up, this first Spanish feature helmed by two women sidesteps the over-earnestness or high camp that hallmark so much gay-themed Hispanic cinema, and also provides the best showcase so far for actress-to-watch Leonor Watling. Released in mid-January to better-than-expected opening biz, pic can expect to find a home in gay fests, but its basic troubled-romance motif could potentially appeal to a broader audience base."

Jonathan Holland *Variety*

CAST OF CHARACTERS

Leonor Watling (Elvira); Rosa María Sardà (Sofia); María Pujalte (Jimena); Silvia Abascal (Sol); Eliska Sirová (Eliska); Chisco Amado (Miguel); Xabier Elorriaga (Carlos); Álex Angulo (Bernardo); Aitor Mazo (Ernesto); Sergio Otegui (Javier); Fernando Colomo (Juez de Paz)

My Wife Maurice

Written by Jean-Marie Poiré and Raffy Shart.
Directed by Jean-Marie Poiré.
Produced by Jean-Marie Poiré and Igor Sekulic.
Released by Comedie Star
in association with TLA Releasing.
www.mafemmesappellemaurice.com
Genre: Adventure/Comedy
Runtime: 102 Minutes
French with English subtitles

PLOT SYNOPSIS:
Emmanuelle is foiled in her plan to wed George, whom she perceives as a millionaire. Learning he's got another wife who is in charge of the euros, she plans to contact her and tell her what Georgie boy has been up to. Hoping to save himself from ruin, George pressures a man, Maurice, into dressing up in drag and pretending to be his wife. The fun is just beginning in the French farce.

As has been suggested, this adventure/comedy is like a *La Cage aux Folles* written by an author on acid. First, the plot. Emmanuelle, rather cleverly acted by Alice Evans, is on the verge of achieving her greatest ambition, which is to marry George Audefey, as played by Philippe Chevallier. In her dreams, he'll take her to the top.

In Venice she learns that he's already married and that all his money actually belongs to his wife, Marion, as played by Virginie Lemoine.

Götz Otto and Régis Laspalés

Emmanuelle decides she'll expose their relationship to George's wife, hoping that as an act of revenge she'll ruin the two-timer's life for good.

Totally desperate, and under immense blackmail pressure, George seeks out Maurice Lappin, as played by Régis Laspalés. Maurice, who is a poor volunteer, collects clothes for a charity in Montmartre. He is assigned the task of dressing up in drag and pretending to be George's wife. George hopes that this will scare off Emmanuelle.

From George's ludicrous idea arise a series of blunders and catastrophes, beginning with the arrival of Emmanuelle's jealous and randy boyfriend, Johnny Zucchini (a name you'll love), played grotesquely by Götz Otto.

By now the plot is really rolling as we look in on this Eurotrash, featuring everything from bearded drag queens to women with chainsaws.

Alice Evans

Régis Laspalés

PRODUCTION CREW:

Director of Photography: Robert Alazraki
Music: Yuri Buenaventura, Pierre Charvet, and Vincent
                        Prezioso
Editors: Jean-Marie Poiré and Henry Revlou
Production Designer: Katia Wyszkop
Costume Designer: Olivier Bériot
Production Management: Jean-Philippe Avenel, Sonja Döring, Olivier
                        Hélie, and Olivier Lüer
Assistant Directors: Eric Bartonio, Jean-Christophe Delpias, Olivier
                        Horlait, Andreas Meszaros, and Alexandre
                        Schmitt

WHAT THE CRITICS SAID:

"A heavy-handed vaudeville comedy spun around adultery, cross-dressing and mistaken identities, *My Wife Maurice* is a gamely thesped, lowbrow farce. Adapted from a long-running stage hit – the biggest legit draw in Gaul after *La Cage aux Folles* – pic is helmed with a sledgehammer and full of yucks that all issue from the cuckold-and-banana-peel school of humor."

Lisa Nesselson *Variety*

"After a Venetian getaway devolves into a male horror fantasy, with Emmanuelle nearly incinerating his genitals with a crème brûlée torch, Georges escapes to his Montmartre pad. When Emmanuelle calls, toting a chainsaw, he enlists the help of Maurice (Régis Laspalés), the persistent charity-worker on his doorstep, who disguises himself *La Cage aux Folles*-style as Georges's wife."

Kris Wilton *Village Voice*

"Slap an ill-fitting dress on an ugly man and you have instant guffaws. That surefire vaudeville tactic guarantees the chaotic French farce *My Wife Maurice* a fair share of laughs. Who can resist the ridiculous spectacle of a bearded, middle-aged salesman in drag waving his chubby arms and clomping around like the world's clumsiest ballerina?"

Stephen Holden *New York Times*

"The two main actors give it their best shot, and the movie cracks along at a brisk pace. Gag follows gag, and Laspalés is very funny as the irritating, obsessive Maurice. Poiré's comedy often pushed the definition of good taste to its limit. Numerous French actors lend their services – Anemone, Paul Belmondo, Virginie Lemoine, Guy Marchand, Stephane Audran."

Judith Prescott *Hollywood Reporter*

"Though not overtly homosexual in theme, the perfect comic timing, witty dialogue and sense of Eurocamp make this cross-dressing farce a heterosexual *La Cage aux Folles* with heaving bosoms. Strap yourself in and enjoy the ride."

Darren Chadwick *TLA Releasing*

CAST OF CHARACTERS

Alice Evans (Emmanuelle); Régis Laspalés (Maurice Lappin); Philippe Chevallier (Georges Audefey); Götz Otto (Johnny Zucchini); Anémone (Claire Trouabal); Martin Lamotte (Jean-Bernard Trouabal); Virginie Lemoine (Marion Audefey); Guy Marchand (Charles Boisdain); Urbain Cancelier (Poilard); Stéphane Audran (Jacqueline Boisdain); Marco Bonini (Le pientre vénitien); Michéle Garcia (La vendeuse de prêt-á-porter); Sylvie Joly (La femme dans Orlyval); Raphaël Mezrahi (Le type au defile de mode)

Proteus

Written and Directed by John Greyson
and Jack Lewis
Produced by Anita Lee, Stephen Makovitz,
and Platon Trakoshis
A Big World Cinema/Pluck Production
in association with Idol Pictures
Distributed by Strand Releasing
www.proteusthemovie.com
Genre: Drama/Romance
Runtime: 100 Minutes

PLOT SYNOPSIS:
In this joint Canadian/South African film, most of the action transpires during the early 18th century on Robben Island, Cape Town's penal colony. It tells the story of two lovers—one a Dutch sailor in prison for sodomy, the other a young herdsman from the Hottentot tribe. Attracted to each other, the prisoners begin an affair, breaking the cultural taboos of both homosexuality and interracial love. Based on a true story as recorded in 18th century court transcripts, the condemned pair face their doom together, finding a safe union only in death at sea.

This film originated with the fascination its director felt for the story of two Dutch-speaking prisoners during the early 18th century in what is today known as South Africa. It's a tale about forbidden love during an era when sodomy was judged as worse than murder, and it's a story that illuminates the institutionalized extermination of men engaged in homosexual acts by a moralistic penal code. Complicating the story was the fact that within European society at the time, interracial love was virtually unthinkable, and that the protagonists in this drama included a white and a black man.

Neil Sandilands and Rouxnet Brown

The screenplay was based on South African court records that were meticulously compiled during the trial of Rijkhaart Jacobsz (a white Dutch sailor imprisoned in the 1720s for sodomy) and Claas Blank (a Hottentot tribesman accused but never convicted of cattle theft). Each of them was incarcerated within South Africa's most notorious penal colony, Robben Island. (Ironically, Robben Island, was the much later site of Nelson Mandela's life sentence.)

After lengthy trials, the details of which were meticulously recorded in archaic Dutch script that linguists, including the modern-day Dutch themselves, have difficulty interpreting, they were jointly sentenced to death for their "crimes" by being bound together with chains and pushed off the edge of a ship.

As the film depicts, the men's incarceration occurred during an era when Calvinists and/or vengefully hysterical moralists controlled most of northern European society. Adding to the self-righteous indignation of the South African court was a repressive policy in Amsterdam at the time. (It's hard to believe that swinging Amsterdam was ever this repressive, but that's one of the lessons inherent in this film.) There, early in the 18th century, more than 70 accused sodomites were executed on Dam Square. One of them, according to the film, was the former lover of the married and much-repressed administrator of Robben Island, a character whose affection and obsession for the black prisoner, Blank, at first helps the prisoner, and then fatally adds to the power of his accusers.

This film encompasses concepts that go way beyond the thwarted love between two men. It emerges as a historical document that unveils not only the individual travails of Rijkhaart Jacobsz and Claas Blank, but the sweeping condemnation of gays throughout the Dutch-speaking colonial world, in circumstances that often led to public humiliation, imprisonment, and eventually, death. Documents uncovered by the filmmakers revealed the trials of tens of thousands of mainly black men in colonial South Africa, many of them for sodomy, and many of them leading to executions as late as the 1870s.

The filmmakers were helped by the meticulous attention that local prosecutors at the time spent on the compilation and recording of their evidence. One case they uncovered involved a Dutch sailor and two slaves who were caught in a shared sex act while crossing the Atlantic. All three of them were dumped on Robben Island, where they were caught in sex acts again and later executed. But the case of Claas Blank and Rijkhaart Jacobsz stands out above the other recorded cases because of the length of their association—more than 17 years (call it love?). In the film version, the length of their involvement was reduced to a more manageable 10 years.

The movie is a bitter and alarming reminder that gay people have paid a high price for their sexual orientation. Especially poignant is the inability, or unwillingness, of the accused to even give a name to the feelings that one or the other might have had for the other. As the filmmakers painfully convey, homosexual acts had (highly pejorative) names at the time, but perhaps because of a lack of role models, homosexuals themselves usually had only a limited ability to put their feelings and desires into any broad perspective. Thus, the two prisoners are each painfully inarticulate about their thoughts and feelings. As noted in their abbreviated and cryptic comments to the court, neither of them benefited from a shared vocabulary that described their condition, and their executioners noted that nothing particularly insightful was expressed even a few moments prior to their joint execution. Chained together, they died by simultaneous drowning in Table Bay, whose waters quickly swallowed them up as the camera films a scene of otherwise stunning natural beauty. Except for the efforts of the filmmakers of *Proteus*, the fate of Rijkhaart and Claas, and the fate of hundreds of other "sodomites"--both genuine and those falsely accused--would have gone forever unheralded and unrecorded.

104

Creative Anachronisms
and Dutch Frugality

Aware that the repressive policies of South Africa spanned almost 300 years of colonial history (and equally aware of the expense that would have been involved if they had insisted on chronological integrity of costumes and settings), the filmmakers--for budgetary reasons--maintained an artfully offhanded attitude about accuracy of period furnishings, costumes, and settings.

The scary-looking officer dragging the emaciated 18th-century convicts off to a water-torture cell might be wearing the khaki-colored police uniform of South Africa in the 1960s. The misunderstood wife of the closeted and sexually repressed colonial governor might preside over her 18th century salon in a sleeveless, knee-length cocktail dress that might have been appropriate at an *haute-bourgeoise* midsummer dinner party in The Hague. The hideaway where the 18th-century sexual coupling (and presumably some of the emotional bonding) of the two prisoners was filmed was a rust-stained, concrete-sided water tower belonging to Vergenoegd Farm, in the Somerset West district of modern-day South Africa.

Sometimes these anachronisms seem jarring; at other times they reinforce an overview of the Jacobsz-Blank affair as a single episode within the larger context of the evolution of South Africa itself.

The film's most compelling, and perhaps its most brilliant, anachronism involves three working-class, modern-day Dutch stenographers whose job involves recording the archaic Dutch language used by the early 18th-century court in its interrogation of the prisoners. Bashing out their transcripts on circa 1960s IBM typewriters, cracking bubble gum, chain-smoking, gossiping about their private lives, and making frequent re-arrangements to their beehive coiffures, they stop their work frequently to listen and—with the help of Dutch-language dictionaries—to interpret the court's terse, abbreviated, and archaic vocabulary and word usage. And in ways that reflect the overall dismay felt by the film's audience, the Dutch-speaking stenographers complain about their difficulties in translating the statements of both the defendants and their oppressors. One of them even expresses regret at the court's ability to twist human affection and sexuality into a revolutionary crime against society.

This artfully anachronistic device reinforced the difficulty of resurrecting a human drama from the abbreviated legalese of another era. It's also a lesson about the degree to which anti-gay oppression can become part of the legal fabric of this and any age.

And the beat goes on.

Rouxnet Brown

Kristen Thomson

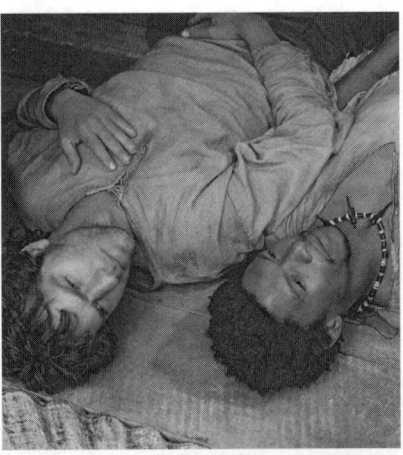
Neil Sandilands and Rouxnet Brown

PRODUCTION CREW:

Director of Photography: Giulio Biccari
Music: Don Pyle and Andrew Zealley
Editor: Roslyn Kalloo
Production Designer: Tom Hannam
Costume Designer: Diana Cilliers

WHAT THE CRITICS SAID:

"This Canadian/South African production tells the story of illicit love among men imprisoned off the coast of South Africa in the early 18th century. Two of the men— a Dutch sailor and an African herder—have a sexual relationship that they try to keep a secret. Meanwhile, the botanist in charge of the prison garden takes an interest in the herder. Though married, the botanist is happiest when he's with the prisoner, lecturing him about the finer points of flowers. One doesn't have to have a green thumb to get the sneaking suspicion that all the dialogue about pistols and stamen and plants that bloom at night could be alluding to more than flora."
     G. Allen Johnson, Ruthe Stein, and John McMurtrie *San Francisco Chronicle*

"The story merges gender politics and imperialist practice into an ideologically meaty whole."

Dave Kehr *The New York Times*

"The film spends much of its running time depicting the physical encounters between the two prisoners, presented in a soft-core erotic fashion that wouldn't be out of place on late-night cable."

Frank Scheck *The Hollywood Reporter*

"Though Greyson and Lewis have condensed the couple's 17 years into a decade, they do convey how lust can flower into a deep and abiding love. Although homosexuality is punishable by death under Dutch law, the prison's administrators largely look the other way. But as has been the case throughout history, governments come down hard on gays when it serves their interests; Claas and Rijkhaart are at all times vulnerable."

Kevin Thomas *Los Angeles Times*

CAST OF CHARACTERS

Rouxnet Brown (Claas Blank); Brett Goldin (Lourens); Tessa Jubber (Elize); Jeroen Kranenburg (Scholz); Dean Lotz (Governor); Kwanda Malunga (Claas age 10); Terry Norton (Betsy); Adrienne Pierce (Tinnie); Jane Rademeyer (Niven's Wife); Neil Sandilands (Rijkhaart Jacobsz); Shaun Smyth (Virgil Niven); Grant Swansby (Willer); Kristen Thomson (Kate)

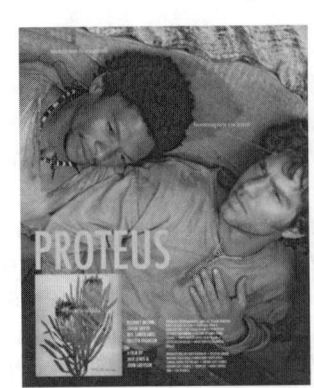

The Raspberry Reich

Written and Directed by Bruce La Bruce
Produced by: Jürgen Brüning
Released by Strand Releasing.
www.strandreleasing.com
Genre: Comedy/Drama
Runtime: 90 Minutes
German with English subtitles

PLOT SYNOPSIS:
A critique of terrorist chic from pop culture maverick Bruce La Bruce.

Andreas Rupprecht and Anton Z. Risan

The Raspberry Reich is a film about "radical chic," specifically the phenomenon of the modern left in Germany adopting the signifiers and postures of extreme left-wing movements of the 1970s, particularly the Red Army Faction, also known as the Baader-Meinhoff Gang.

The movie starts off with the abduction by a gang of bumbling, would-be terrorists of Patrick, a young man who is the son of one of the wealthiest bankers in Germany. A scene of chaos and slapstick humor ensues in which Clyde, one of the aspiring terrorists--or activists, as they prefer to call themselves-- accidentally handcuffs himself to the kidnapping victim and is forced to join him in the trunk of their stolen BMW.

Unbeknownst to the rest of the gang, Clyde, whose job it is to follow Patrick and report his whereabouts to his cohorts, has already enjoyed a sexual liaison with Patrick, and even in advance of the abduction, the two young men are already planning Patrick's escape. The gang does not realize that Patrick's father disowned and disinherited him when Patrick came out to the world at large as being gay, and therefore he has no value as a hostage. Nothing seems to go right for this idealistic but ineffectual gang of aspiring terrorists.

In the meantime, the leader of the Raspberry Reich, Gudrun, a charismatic young woman who has patterned herself after Gudren Ensslin, one of the main members of the Baader-Meinhoff Gang, has indoctrinated the other members of the gang to her cause. Gudrun, a strict devotee of Wilhelm Reich and Herbert Marcuse, believes that heterosexual monogamy is a bourgeois conceit that must be smashed in order to achieve True Revolution. To that end, she forces her straight male followers to have sex with each other to prove their mettle as authentic revolutionaries. When Holger, one of her followers, protests that he is her boyfriend, Gudrun tells him not to be ridiculous, that The Revolution is her boyfriend.

Gudrun is constantly preaching her revolutionary rhetoric to the impressionable young men in her entourage, but she often finds it difficult to live up to the extreme ideals by which she attempts to govern her life and the lives of her followers.

After having sex in a public elevator with Holger and visiting the shooting range with Andreas, Gudrun starts to hatch her hostage scheme in order to extort money from Patrick's father, which she plans to distribute to the oppressed, impoverished working class, and also to draw attention to their glamorous cause. Unfortunately for Gudrun, Clyde and Patrick have ambitions of their own. They eventually escape and become bank robbers, stealing money from one of the banks owned by Robert's father.

After the terrorists' plot is foiled, the film traces what becomes of each of the members. Helmut and Horst, who were previously straight, become gay lovers. They run into Andreas, who seems to be in the closet, in a gay bar on an evening that has a terrorist chic theme. Che, another member of the gang, who patterns himself after Che Guevara, moves to the Middle East, where he begins to train real terrorists in the methodolgies of kidnappings. Sometimes those who indulge radical chic do become real--and dangerous--terrorists. And of course Gudrun and Holger get married, have a child, and become members of the bourgeoisie, although Gudrun still pays lip service to her radical beliefs.

Our Favorite Musical Moment

Within a riveting but disjointed few minutes into the film, Gudrun and her boyfriend, in front of larger-than-life replica of Che Guevara, decide to make love. On the other side of the paper-thin wall, another of their Marxist colleagues masturbates while licking and sucking on the barrel of a (presumably loaded) pistol. During foreplay, we hear the languorous sounds of the string section, presumably of the Berlin Philharmonic, tuning up. The foreplay/tune-up is followed by a musical and sexual crescendo, suitably Wagnerian. Even the moments immediately before and after orgasm are accompanied with Marxist-Leninist rhetoric and lots of info about what really happened to the imprisoned members of the Bader-Meinhoff gang after their arrests in the 1970s.

Bader Meinhoff and the New Sexual Chic
(Marxist-Leninist Ideologies for the Horny)

Gudrun, the heroine of this film, and the way she describes revolutionary socialism and the sexual revolution, make for some of the most memorable scenes. Nubile and Aryan, the physical ideal of the Third Reich, she evokes a sex-crazed Walkyrian on an ideological rampage, the subject of the erotic dreams of heterosexual males (and gay women) everywhere. Only until you're about ten minutes into the film will you realize that her phraseologies are brilliant pastiches of radical politics blended with the politics of sexual liberation. Some are so memorable that we've compiled "the handbook of Gudrun-isms" as a means of publicizing this film's blend of satire, irony, and political/sexual extremeism.

GUDRUN: As a setting for sex, sheets, mattresses, even the bedroom itself are merely instruments of bourgeois capitalist oppression. So I want you to fuck me NOW, here, standing up.

GUDRUN (Speaking to a nearby, presumably heterosexual male about their latest kidnapping victim): There will be no revolution without sexual revolution, and there will be no sexual revolution without homosexual revolution. Therefore, as a means of liberating yourself from your bourgeois capitalistic repression, kiss the captive, and make love to him. NOW!"

NEARBY MALE, responding to Gudrun: But Gudrun, I am your boyfriend.
GUDRUN: You are not my boyfriend! The Revolution is my boyfriend!

Director's Notes: Porno and Sexual Politics

The Raspberry Reich is an art/porno film that, like all of my films, uses pornography as a starting point to examine sexual politics and homosexual radicalism. (For me, working in pornography is like a genre exercise.) Like my previous two films, *Hustler White* and *Skin Flick*, *The Raspberry Reich* concerns an all-male gang that does not strictly identify itself as homosexual, but whose members nonetheless are sexually active with each other. Each of the movies examines identity politics, emphasizing that homosexual identity is fluid and can be separated from a strict gay politic. In *The Raspberry Reich*, Gudrun initiates the sexual dynamic between the heterosexual males who idolize her; she recognizes the innate radical potential of homosexual expression and attempts to manipulate it toward her revolutionary ends.

The fact that she is constantly quoting Reich and Marcuse is no coincidence: the RAF and other radical movements of the seventies believed in the sexually revolutionary ideals of these post-Freudian thinkers, and fought against all forms of sexual repression and the constraints of gender. It is essential that my film engage these notions with sexually explicit content, for in this way it mirrors all the sexual ambivalence and ambiguities of the radical movements that emerged in the sixties which are now being revived in art and fashion, but which could soon become a new social and political force in modern culture.

Susanne Sachsse

Daniel Batscher, Andreas Rupprecht, and Daniel Moller

OTHER DIVINELY REVOLUTIONARY GUDRUN-ISMS:

Heterosexuality is the opiate of the masses!

Homosexuality is the highest form of class struggle!

Make (revolutionary) love, not (imperialistic) war!

Don't question authority: Eradicate it!

CAST OF CHARACTERS

Susanne Sachsse (Gudrun); Daniel Batscher (Holger); Andreas Rupprecht (Patrick); Dean Stathis (Andreas); Anton Z. Risan (Clyde); Daniel Fettig (Che); Gerrit (Helmut); Joeffrey (Horst); Ulrike S. (Neighbor 1); Sherry Vine (Drag Queen Stage); Punktchen (Drag Queen Door); Sven Reinhard (Police Man); Genesis P. Orridge (TV Personality); Naushad (Muslim); Huseyin Gunis (Arab Terrorist 1); Alfredo Holz (Arab Terrorist 2); Claus Matthes (Arab Terrorist 3); Rafael Caba (Arab Terrorist 4); Mischika Kral (Diplomat); Marco Volk (Chauffeur); Darius Sautter Aschkanpour (Baby); Andreas Stadler (Voice Che); Ralf Grawe (Voice Helmut); Mario Mentrup (Voice Horst); Christoph Glaubacker (Voice Patrick)

WHAT THE CRITICS SAID:

"It's hard to know who exactly the audience for this sort of fare is, since even the most adventurous art house patrons are likely to be put off by the nonstop sex and those looking for other kinds of stimulation aren't likely to want to put up with the film's subversive humor, as occasionally witty as it is. Still, one has to admire the filmmaker for his sheer audacity and willingness to push the stylistic envelope."

Frank Scheck *The Hollywood Reporter*

"Vet Canadian film *bad boy* (though that designation is getting pretty age inappropriate now) Bruce La Bruce goes to Germany but is otherwise up to his usual tricks with *The Raspberry Reich*, his second self-labeled *porno*. The ostensible proof of radical chic is, like his previous works, at once amusingly outrageous and slightly dull. Graphic sex acts will make an already marginal vid-shot item tough to place beyond gay-fests, underground venues and specialized home-format sales, though purportedly an R-rated version is also in the works."

Dennis Harvey *Variety*

"With puzzling electro-punk music and strobing pink slogans, the film merrily sends up Patty Hearst's captors, the fuzzy logic of anarchists and the monkey-see, monkey-do slavishness of true believers. Gudrun orders the butchest of her bunch to lie down with the most curious, who had earlier enjoyed an indescribable autoerotic moment with a pistol. Her charge balks, protesting that he was her boyfriend. 'The Revolution is my boyfriend!' she insists, in a slogan that winds up on her T-shirt, then on those of her would-be terrorists, and soon enough, across the pecs of bemused La Bruce fans.

Mr. La Bruce has been called the John Waters of Canada, and on this day, when Mr. Waters comes out with his taboo-pushing Charm City farce, *Dirty Shame*, there seem to be few lines left to cross on film. As Mr. Waters has noted, penetration is the final frontier, the last gasp for any shockable moviegoers still out there. This ribald outrage, although it belongs to a very specific group of supporters, inches that agenda forward."

Ned Martel *The New York Times*

PRODUCTION CREW:

Director of Photography: James Carmen
Editor: Jorn Hartmann
Costume Designer: Lunder Wekenborg

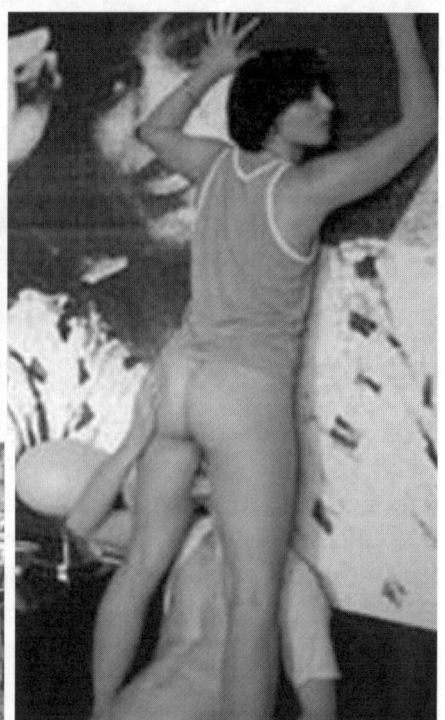

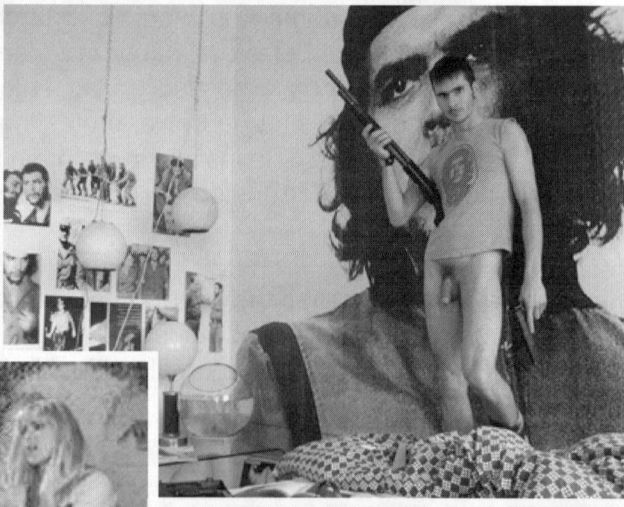

She Hate Me

Written by Michael Genet.
Directed by Spike Lee.
Produced by Jean Cazes
and Jamal Debbouze.
Released by 40 Acres and a Mule
in association with Sony Pictures Classics.
www.shehateme.com
Genre: Comedy/Drama
Runtime: 138 Minutes

PLOT SYNOPSIS:
A biotech executive, John Henry (Jack) Armstrong, is in need of a job. He finds a new business when Fatima, a high-powered business-woman and his former girl-friend – now a lesbian – asks him to impregnate her and her new girlfriend, Alex. The word is out: Jack enters the baby-making business at $10,000 a load. From this point on, especially because his former employers are trying to frame him for secu-rity fraud, Jack's life gets very complicated.

This is the story of a corporate whistleblower turned stud in Spike Lee's new film. Of course, that's too simple an explanation. It's almost like two movies in one. On one front, it's an indictment of corporate culture in America. On another front, it's about a semen-factory stud who impregnates lesbians at $10,000 a pop.

There are other "fronts" as well – or even affronts. This movie didn't please everyone.

Dania Ramirez and Kerry Washington

Roger Ebert wrote one of the most sensitive reviews. He called it "audacious and reck-lessly risky." He said that Lee was "like a juggler who starts out with balls and gradu-ally adds baseball bats, top hats, and chainsaws. It's not an intellectual experience, but an emotional one." Spike Lee defended his film, saying it's about "sex, greed, money, and politics." He found inspiration in recent events involving such corporations as Halliburton or Enron.

"These corporations have some shaky people at the top. I decided to pair that line of inquiry with the idea of sex and procreation. A volatile mixture. The film is also a com-mentary on the hypocrisy of America on the issue of sex. I wanted to raise questions about the decline of morals and ethics in America – from the boardroom to the bed-room."

And so he did, somewhat admirably.

Kerry Washington and Anthony Mackie

Monica Bellucci

PRODUCTION CREW:

Director of Photography:	Matthew Libatique
Producers:	Spike Lee, Jean Cazes, Jamel Debbouze, Preston L. Holmes, Craig M. Spitzer, and Fernando Sulichin
Music:	Terence Blanchard and Raul Midon
Editor:	Barry Alexander Brown
Production Designer:	Brigitte Broch
Costume Designer:	Donna Berwick
Production Management:	Caroline Cochaux, Colin Cumberbatch, and David Pomier

CAST OF CHARACTERS

Anthony Mackie (John Henry 'Jack' Armstrong); Kerry Washington (Fatima Goodrich); Ellen Barkin (Margo Chadwick); Monica Bellucci (Simona Bonasera); Jim Brown (Geronimo Armstrong); Ossie Davis (Judge Buchanan); Jamel Debbouze (Doak); Brian Dennehy (Chairman Billy Church); Woody Herrelson (Leland Powell); Ling Bai (Oni); Lonette McKee (Lottie Armstrong); Paula Jai Parker (Evelyn); Q-tip (Vada Huff); Dania Ramirez (Alex Guerrero); John Turturro (Don Angelo Bonasera)

WHAT THE CRITICS SAID:

"The feisty New York filmmaker with a nose for tabloid news has always relished playing provocateur and setting brushfires with his rub-your-face-in-it style of riffing off the headlines. Usually his rampages leave behind at least some patches of scorched earth before burning out. Throughout *She Hate Me* you can sense Mr. Lee trying to do the right thing. But in spite of itself, the movie supports the adolescent caveman fantasy that a lesbian is really a heterosexual woman who hasn't received proper stud service."

Stephen Holden *New York Times*

"Defenders of this movie will argue that the zip and crackle of Lee's technique are themselves worth the price of a ticket; that only with such freakish energy can a director hope to meet the outrages visited upon the body politic; and that it takes somebody of Lee's nerve to raise one of the most grubby of racial prejudices – the belief that African-American men are prodigal with their paternity – and then not merely dramatize it but defend it. And defend it Lee does."

Anthony Lane *New Yorker*

"Indeed, clever Fatima is soon pimping reluctant Jack to a long line of mainly lipstick lezzies, and he's popping Viagra to keep up with the demand. Sweetback, Super Fly, and Stagolee have nothing on this dude. Not only is Lee's super-stud able to handle (and at least temporarily reprogram) five or six ladies a night, but his super stuff is apparently guaranteed to knock them up every time. "Your sperm just met my egg," coos one satisfied customer, a Mafia princess played by a jetlagged Monica Bellucci."

J. Hoberman *Village Voice*

"Throughout the film, Jack is visited by dozens of mostly attractive gay women, none of whom has apparently heard of artificial insemination or adoption; they approach him with a combination of carnal cynicism, alpha-girl bossiness and orgasmic ecstasy. If Lee is trying to make a political point, it's sloppy. By the time viewers are subjected to a gratuitous soft-lensed flashback of Jack discovering his fiancée in bed with another woman, it's clear that he's more intent on titillating than theorizing."

Ann Hornaday *Washington Post*

"But little does Jack suspect that Fatima will spread the word about his "services" to a network of upwardly mobile lesbians. Soon, Fatima begins making nightly visits to Jack's apartment, with four or five multiculti friends in tow, all willing to ante up for an intimate session with Fatima's ex. Lee then proceeds to show Jack in action, in several montages of uproarious bedroom encounters. Finally, Jack has fathered a whopping 19 offspring. It's a clever reversal of roles – the man as the sex object – but it loses some of its edge because of its cliché depiction of Fatima and her entourage as uniformly baby-feverish man-eaters. Lee and Genet employ lesbianism as a kind-of metaphor for feminism, which may open pic to criticism."

Scott Foundas *Variety*

Showboy

Written and directed by Christian Taylor
and Lindy Heymann.
Released by Fite Films and Here! Films
and Regent Releasing.
www.showboymovie.com
Genre: Comedy
Runtime: 93 Minutes

PLOT SYNOPSIS:
Christian Taylor, playing himself, is a writer for **Six Feet Under***, the hit TV series. A British documentary crew is profiling him when he's fired. The crew follows him to Las Vegas where he attempts to become a dancer, although he has "the wrong body."*

Adrian Armas and Christian Taylor

This comedy, with touches of drama, calls itself a "faction," meaning that it's part mock documentary, part reality. Well, sort of reality. One viewer from Bucharest called it a "mockumentary." The premise is a bit far-fetched, but the directors handle that problem by advertising their film as, "No dream is crazy if you want to live it."

In this case the dream resides in the head of Christian Taylor, who directed and co-authored the film. In real life, he is actually a writer-producer for the HBO hit, *Six Feet Under*, one of the better shows on television these days. In the film (not in real life), he's fired from the series by his show's creator, Alan Ball. This occurs just at the time a British TV crew is doing a documentary on Christian. The TV crew is headed by Heymann, who, along with Christian, co-authored and co-directed the film. Even though fired, Christian persuades Heymann to record his continuing adventures in Las Vegas where he has gone to audition as a chorus boy. Heymann and her crew dutifully film the embarrassing results of his pursuit.

Nature did not intend for Christian to be a showboy. For one thing, he's "too old." Christian is in his 30's. For another, he's too short at 5 feet, 9 inches, to dance in the chorus line. Producers want tall, ripped showboys, and Christian is beginning to develop a pudge. The "hint" of a protruding stomach drives Christian to investigate liposuction. At this point, the film is at its most effective in recording the humiliations a performer encounters in show business, including the inevitable put-downs where one's entire body is often rejected.

In Vegas, Christian settles in to the home of a former acquaintance, Erich Miller, appearing in the film as an ex-chorus boy.
In his attempts to become a showboy, Christian encounters two Vegas legends, Siegfried & Roy, who discover that as a dancer he can't do splits. We could laugh more

at the shallow qualities of Siegfried & Roy were it not for their subsequent heartbreaking tragedy. Even Whoopi Goldberg, the nemesis of the extreme right, puts in an appearance, playing her role as herself rather sincerely. She offers to put Christian in to contact with "Boylesque show." Later, he auditions as male stripper.

The film scores some points in depicting the loneliness and alienation gays experience, two qualities that can feed self-absorption. While hardly the greatest show biz film ever made, it does it better than some of those cheesy "reality" programs on television these days.

It's obvious that both Lindy Heymann and especially Christian Taylor approached their material with a lot of sincerity and dedication to their project. At this simplest level, it is fun to look on as Christian sets out on a series of embarrassments, hoping to propel himself in the high-kicking chorus line of tall, ripped pretty boys, who inhabit Vegas by the hundreds.

Perhaps the unanswered question is why Christian, with no former experience in dancing, wants to pursue such a thankless career in a world inhabited by the shallow and the glitzy.

Apparently, Christian had a childhood dream to be a showboy. If there's a moral to this film, it's that we should tread lightly into that good night when following our dreams of yesterday. Reality might intrude on those dreams, especially for anyone contemplating a career in show business.

Of course, most of us know that already.

| Christian Taylor | Lindy Heymann | Jason Buchtel | Adrian Armas |

PRODUCTION CREW:

Director of Photography: Joaquin Baca-Asay
Music: Daniele Luppi
Editor: Kant Pan
Sound Department: Matthew Gough and David Wyman
Production Management: Cara DiPaolo

WHAT THE CRITICS SAID:

"Taylor takes an amusingly detached look at himself and his predicaments, but that he is so striking and charismatic drives home all the more acutely just how isolated even the most personable gay man can feel--and by extension, how isolated anyone can feel. Because *Showboy* has such a light, witty touch, the serious chord it strikes resonates all the more deeply."

Kevin Thomas *Los Angeles Times*

"The film's actors are often shot in silhouette, against Vegas' incessant sun, heat, and neon. Ultimately, though, Heymann and Taylor seem to want to have its acid-tinged cake and eat it too, and the film feels soft around the edges, like a chorus boy who'd never make the cut."

Variety

"The subject of the film, and its co-director, is Christian Taylor, a writer for the HBO series "Six Feet Under" who is supposedly being profiled for a documentary by British filmmaker Lindy Heymann. Just as she begins shooting, "Six Feet Under" creator Alan Ball fires Taylor from the series, though Taylor doesn't realize that Heymann knows it. Telling her that he's taken a leave, he heads to Vegas to do "research" for an upcoming project involving male dancers, in the process attempting to become one himself.

The resulting humiliations -- he's 5-foot-9 and not exactly a prime physical specimen -- form the principal comic elements of the film, which documents his rather ridiculous attempts to whip himself into shape and convince highly skeptical prospective employers that he belongs onstage. Among the real-life show business figures appearing in brief cameos are a seemingly sincere Whoopi Goldberg and Siegfried & Roy; the latter's appearance would have been far more amusing if not for subsequent events."

Frank Scheck *Hollywood Reporter*

CAST OF CHARACTERS

Christian Taylor (Writer "Christian"); Lindy Heymann (Director "Lindy"); Marilyn Milgrom (London Producer "Marilyn"); Joe Daley (roommate Joe); Erich Miller (Showboy "Erich"); Jason Buchtel (Vegas Producer "Jason"); Aaron Porter (Dance Instructor); Adrian Armas (Model/Dancer "Adrian"); Billy Sameth (Close friend "Billy"); Lauren Amrose (Herself); Alan Ball (Himself); Alan Connell (Himself); Frances Conroy (Herself); Siegfried Fischbacher (Himself); Whoopi Goldberg (Herself); Rachel Griffiths (Herself); Michael C. Hall (Himself); Roy Horn (Himself); Peter Krause (Himself); Freddy Rodriguez (Himself); Jeremy Sisto (Himself)

Cameos Galore

Siegfried Fischbacher

Whoopi Goldberg

Roy Horn

The Singing Forest

Written, directed, and produced by Jorge Ameer.
Released by Hollywood Independents
in association with A.J. Productions.
www.hollywoodindependents.com
Genre: Drama, Fantasy, Romance
Runtime: 72 minutes

PLOT SYNOPSIS:
Friends and lovers, each forced to wear pink triangles, are brutally murdered in anti-gay pogroms during the Holocaust. Both reincarnate under different circumstances in this modern-day fairy tale about death, reincarnation, and the enduring (and unpredictable) powers of love.

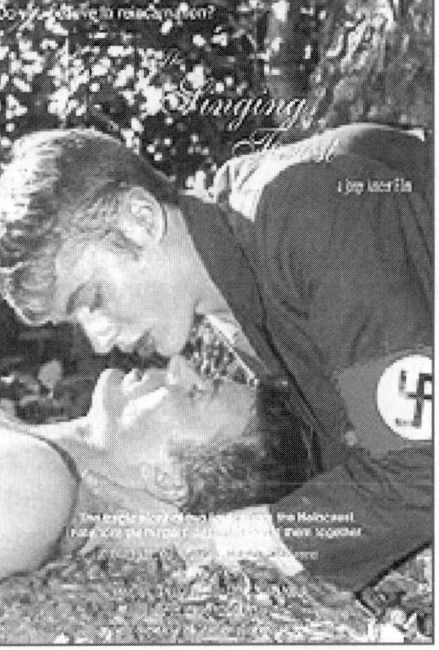

John Sherrin and Craig Pinkston

Stylish and artful, this film by Jorge Ameer pulls its viewers into a free-associative ride that incorporates two separate eras, at least three (and in some cases as many as five) separate points of view, and references that move fluidly between the people we think we are and the people we might have been in earlier lifetimes.

Symbolism cheerfully weaves its way throughout the narrative in ways that touch on wildly free-associative archetypes: Duets evolve into trios, trios devolve into duets, and, we're warned, that human memories are so subjective that truth is, by definition, variable and intensely personal.

The Singing Forest opens with some of the most daring segués in the history of filmmaking: Tender scenes of gay male-on-male affection during the Weimar Republic alternate with views of emaciated corpses in the death camps at Auschwitz. Time streams forward, backward, and sideways. Some scenes evoke a Dada-istic revival of Alfred Hitchcock: Nazi storm troopers roaring down a staircase, dragging *schwuler* off to be tortured. These alternate with images of modern-day healthy bodies that are bound and bleeding, a forecast of emaciated deaths to come. From there, the plot spins and then thickens around the dynamic of a modern-day southern California family which, while hipper and more evolved than most, is ill-equipped for the conflicting loyalties that evolve when resurrected soulmates are reunited..

During the course of this film, two swift-flowing streams of consciousness run constantly, sometimes in different directions. Good-looking actors deftly switch in and out of alternate realities in patterns that are sometimes synchronized and sometimes not.

Things get complicated when Daddy, the humpy-looking, presumably heterosexual, 50-something father of the bride realizes that the young man that his daughter is about to marry is actually the reincarnation of his male lover from the Weimar Republic. The slow, agonized, and sexually keyed-up discovery of their shared Connection is part of the plot, their pain, and their destiny. Like bodies swimming up from great watery depths, the two (extremely good-looking) protagonists rediscover the love that bound them together during their tragically truncated earlier lives.

After some initial jolts, the viewer is swept up into the fluidity of the time-line, passively charmed by the supple grace of yummy-looking actor (John Sherrin) who might, depending on the scene he's playing at the time, be interpreted as either the tender, loyal and mostly heterosexual father of the bride-to-be, or a marauding sexual predator whose joy at meeting the love of his earlier life is dampened by his guilt about *schtupping* his daughter's fiancé (Craig Pinkston). Complicating matters in a way that pulls him firmly back into his relatively conventional realities in Santa Barbara, are his paralyzing memories about his initial mistreatment (rape, actually) of the woman he later married, spent an uneventful 22 years with, and with whom he fathered a child which, ironically, is named Destiny. Destiny (engagingly played by Erin Leigh Price), in a witty double entendre, becomes the means wherein he's eventually united with the love of his former life.

Adding savor to this percolating stew are the insights of real-life California psychic Toni Zobel, who we relate to alternately as a Santerian priestess, a laid back character actress, and a South California incarnation of the Oracle at Delphi.

When are the moments in this film when we realize, with renewed force, that we're still gay? In this film, it's when Junior, after a scene of engaging vulnerability, announces that he'd like a bagel with cream cheese, fresh strawberries, and coffee. In a collective knee-jerk response, every gay male in the audience feels a sudden urge to begin nurturing. And when blond Daddy, shirtless, buff, and looking like the man we'd most like to fool around with after midnight at a leather convention, talks about the agony of his depression, we even manage to forgive him for how, at 50-something, he looks hotter than most of us ever did at 28. Because of their naturalism and talent that goes way beyond their charm and good looks, the male leads from this film really have you rooting that they'll link into their romantic connections and transform their murky *ménage a trois* into a male-on-male duet.

Thanks to some artfully managed symbolism involving appearances, disappearances, and substitutions at the altar under the watchful eyes of the world's best-looking pastor (Louis Perez; I doubt that he'd remain abstinent for long, at least if this film buff had anything to do with it), the film concludes with the strong intimation that, indeed, the magnetic attraction of rediscovered soulmates from past lives take precedence over today's less compelling *passions de passage*.

Cutest bit player?

Louis Perez, who alas never gets a speaking role, and who's credited as the film's chief grip and electrician, plays a humpy looking pastor who we'd follow on any Crusade.

Cutest bit of "stage business?"

When Daddy barfs after too much false bravado and too much tequila, Junior gets tender. All of it's filmed within the tunnel shot of a camera positioned on the floor of a long and narrow bathroom.

Music?

The music in this film(as sung in Italian by Renato Zero, with additional musical scores by Jose Herring and Pedro Bromfman) is absolutely wonderful. *Vivere!* haunts, llingers, uplifts.

Louis Perez

Craig Pinkston

Erik Morris and Craig Pinkston

PRODUCTION CREW:

Director of Photography: Gary Tachell
Art Direction: Renae Plant
Music: Jose Herring and Pedro Bromfman
Casting: John Jacobs
Editors: Laurence Benedict, L. Black, Kristen Reed, and Michelle Clay
Sound Department: Andy Sowerwine

Erik Morris and Craig Pinkston

WHAT THE CRITICS SAID:

"*The Singing Forest* uses graphic images to convey the horrors of the gay Holocaust, a subject worthy of greater cinematic exploration....There's full frontal nudity and a happy, if fantastical, ending."

The Washington Blade

"Add to the mix a couple of reincarnations and a gay paternal Oedipal plot line and you've got yourself one hell of a bush song!"

Netflix.com

"...with this complicated story line, the actors' performances are developed with excellence."

Michael Mulvaney, *Long Island Community Connection*

"Two gay lovers are killed during the Holocaust, are reincarnated and brought back together in this little indie from writer-director Jorge Ameer, sure to get some attention from its commingling of homosexuality and Nazi imagery."

Dennis Harvey, *Variety*

CAST OF CHARACTERS

John Sherrin (Christopher); Erin Leigh Price (Destiny); Craig Pinkston (Alexander/Ben); Erik Morris (Jo); David Guzzone (Young Christopher); Shelley Price (Savannah); Jorge Ameer (Charlie); Toni Zobel (Psychic); Lance Black (Bill); Sal Roman (Stephen); Marc Ambrose, Randal Craig, Nolo Ortiz, Justin Huddleston, Gregory Saites (Nazi Guards 1,2,3,4, and 5); Emre Ozpirincci, Skyler Thomas (Holocaust Victims 1 and 2); Lisa Marx (Television Guest); Renae Plant (Television Host); Louis Perez (Pastor); Jean Carol (Emily); Gerry Rand (Fred); Colin Campbell (Heinz)

Stage Beauty

Directed by Richard Eyre.
Written by Jeffrey Hatcher.
Produced by Robert DeNiro, Hardy
Justice, Michael Dreyer,
and Jane Rosenthal.
Released by Lions Gate Films
in association with Qwerty Films and
NI European Film Produktions-GMBH &
CO.Kg BBC Films.
www.stagebeautymovie.com
Genre: Drama
Runtime: 110 Minutes

PLOT SYNOPSIS:
Evoking both *A Double Life* and
Shakespeare in Love, Stage Beauty is
set in England in the 1660s.
Puritanical values of that era
demanded that women's roles in the
theater be played by men. Edward
'Ned' Kynaston (Crudup) is
England's most celebrated leading
lady, using his beauty and skill to
make the great female roles his own.
But a few years after Charles II is
restored to the British monarchy, he
allows real women on stage, and
decrees that men may no longer
play women's parts. Virtually
overnight, Ned becomes a virtual
nobody. He contemplates suicide till
his ex-dresser turned actress, Maria
(Claire Danes), makes a man of him
again.

It's worth the price of admission to see Rupert Everett in drag portraying King Charles II and his cross-dressing mistress, Nell Gwynn, as portrayed by Zoe Tapper. In Restoration England, after the return of the monarchy, theater flourished. Except the women's roles were played by men. Ned Kynaston, acted by Billy Crudup, was described by Samuels Pepys in his famous diary as "the most beautiful woman on the London stage."

Ben Chaplin and Billy Crudup

Lusting for him (but is he gay?) is Maria, as interpreted by co-star Claire Danes. She wants to play Desdemona herself, and secretly borrows Ned's costumes and (illegally) moonlights as an actress in a beer-hall production.

Her performance is spied upon and reported to King Charles, who is intrigued at the idea of allowing women on the stage. He is even more intrigued when told that the French had been doing it for years. Regrettably, now that women are allowed to play women, Ned is out of a job.

Richard Eyre's film, *Stage Beauty* was adapted by Jeffrey Hatcher from his play *Compleat Female Stage Beauty*. At its best, although at its simplest, it is the story of two Shakespearean actors in love. In some ways and at a time much later in the world's future, the plight of our hero, Kynaston, suggests the silent screen stars who were forced into oblivion with the coming if the Talkies.

At least we learn one historical secret. How did Nell Gwynn persuade Charles II to ban men from playing women's roles on the English stage?

She gave him a royally sumptuous blow-job.

| Claire Danes | Billy Crudup | Rupert Everett |

PRODUCTION CREW:

Director of Photography:	Andrew Dunn
Executive Producers:	Rachel Cohen, Richard Eyre, Michael Kuhn
	Amir Jacob Malin, and James D. Stern
Music:	George Fenton
Editor:	Tariq Anwar
Production Designer:	Jim Clay
Costume Designer:	Tim Hatley

WHAT THE CRITICS SAID:

"If *Shakespeare in Love* pitted its lovers against harsh and unfair 16th century mores to keep its passion galloping, *Stage Beauty*, which is set in the years after King Charles II gets his throne back after an eighteen year Puritan interregnum, is strictly contemporary in its love thwarting. Tarting itself up in poodle wigs and painted-on beauty marks, the movie playfully blends fact, fiction, and rampant anachronism to explore modern love, the cult of stardom and sexuality as role play.

Watching Kynaston practice his feminine gestures from the wings, Maria imitates him imitating a girl. To see them in action is to know that they don't call them gender roles for nothing.

So, how do you solve a problem like Maria's? She wants to act, but there's no one to teach her. She wants Kynaston, but she wants his job more, This, of course, would present a problem for him: He's about to get cast as Bette Davis in a 17th century production of *All About Eve*."

Carina Chocano Los Angeles Times

"Loads of picturesque Restoration rompery here from the director Richard Eyre, complete with merkins, mascara, autumnally lit tavern interiors and scenes where people scurry past lines of Persil-white washing and squawking chickens."

Peter Bradshaw The Guardian

"The film, written by Jeffrey Hatcher and based on his play, *Compleat Female Stage Beauty,* is really about two things at once: The craft of acting, and the bafflement of love. It must be said that Ned is not a very convincing woman onstage (although he is pretty enough); he plays a woman as a man would play a woman, lacking the natural ease of a woman born to a role. Curiously, when Maria takes over his roles, she also copies his gestures, playing a woman as a woman might play a woman playing a man playing a woman. Only gradually does she relax into herself. 'I've always hated your Desdemona,' she confesses to Ned. 'You never fight, you only die.'"

Roger Ebert

"Those who thought *Shakespeare in Love* was as good as it gets in intelligent costume romantic comedy, will find that director Richard Eyre and writer Jeffrey Hatcher have taken the form to a higher level. Audiences seeking a colorful diversion will leave them with much to talk about afterwards."

Ray Bennett The Hollywood Reporter

WHAT THE CRITICS SAID (CONT'D):

"The mode is comic, if never particularly amusing, dealing in anachronism with the subtlety of *The Flintstones*. Then the film starts to get serious, not to say solemn, as Ned and Maria get up close and personal, talking about gender, sexual identity and the art of acting. It's Tootsie with a periwig and without the jokes. He coaches her as Desdemona and within 42 hours they're ready to shock London with a naturalistic performance of *Othello* that anticipates the RSC and the National Theatre of the latter part of the 20th century and makes Donald Wolfit resemble David Garrick."

Philip French *The Observer*

"*Beauty* will inevitably be compared with the Oscar-winning *Shakespeare in Love*, which unlike *Beauty* had no lulls and a heavier volume of delightful performances. Still, director Richard Eyre and writer Jeffrey Hatcher, who wrote the source play, obviously know the milieu. And Crudup, who seems a bit too muscular for the role, is otherwise a revelation."

Mike Clark *USA Today*

"When Ned and Maria Hughes co-star in *Othello*--Crudup and Danes pair up beautifully--the gender role-playing puts spine in this period piece that is vital to the here and now."

Peter Travers *Rolling Stone*

"Kynaston's Desdemona, all cascading curls and falsetto histrionics, is the talk of the town--but strict boyhood training that stripped his performances of every masculine gesture and intonation has left him sexually confused in his off-stage life, where both men and woman chase him. He is having an affair with his patron, the Duke of Buckingham (Ben Chaplin), but he's also attracted to his dresser, the virginal Maria (Claire Danes). The handsomely shot *Stage Beauty* sometimes teeters on the verge of going completely over the top, but it's mostly saved by its own self-awareness."

Megan Lehmann *New York Post*

"Occasional anachronisms aside, *Stage Beauty* has a weird, compelling energy, fueled by a deliciously dynamic cast, a cheerfully bawdy and odd story line and a refreshing, impossible romance. Its closest relation is *Shakespeare in Love*, but *Stage Beauty* is darker, digging deeper into the maelstrom of male/female role playing on and off stage as well as in and out of bed. It's amusing and, if not exactly romantic, than at least romantically intriguing. It's also the sort of film that will please Shakespeare fanatics, all of whom will get a chuckle at such weary lines as: 'Time to see the Gonerils.'"

Connie Ogle *The Miami Herald*

WHAT THE CRITICS SAID (CONT'D):

"The men in the audience, many of them wearing wigs and barrel bloomers (they're almost in drag themselves), go mad for Kynaston; the women are titillated and entertained. When Charles, eager for excitement, rules that men may no longer play women, Kynaston, whose lover and protector is the Duke of Buckingham, is out of a job; he is replaced by his dresser Maria, who becomes the first English actress to play Desdemona. Crudup stretches himself as Kynaston, but you feel sorry for him. Offstage, people are always pulling off Ned's gown and reaching for Ned's member to see if he's really a man; Maria loves him and climbs into bed with him, which leads to much coy and uneasy tussling over the issue of whether Ned is playing the part of a man or a woman in the sack."

David Denby *The New Yorker*

"At times, the movie feels like a fancy-dress version of *A Star is Born*, with especially tortuous sexual policies. Ned, who specializes in doomed Shakespearean heroines, is a vain and temperamental star, but also a proud and discipline professional. Mr. Crudup's fine features, which flicker between masculine and feminine as the lights flicker and the mood shifts, are well suited for the role, though a sinewy, bird-like frame suggests Hollywood anorexia more than Restoration curves."

A.O Scott *The New York Times*

"The tagline for this movie ought to read: 'It's Shakespeare in Love--
With Everybody!!' "

CAST OF CHARACTERS

Billy Crudup (Ned Kynaston); Claire Danes (Maria); Rupert Everett (King Charles II); Tom Wilkinson (Betterton); Zoe Tapper (Nell Gwynn); Richard Griffiths (Sir Charles Sedley); Ben Chaplin (George Villiars, Duke of Buckingham); Hugh Bonneville (Samuel Pepys); Edward Fox (Sir Edward Hyde); Derek Hutchinson (Stage Manager); Mark Letheren (Male Emilia/Dickie); Jack Kempton (Call Boy); Alice Eve (Miss Frayne); Fenella Woolgar (Lady Meresvale); David Westhead (Harry)

Straight-Jacket

PLOT SYNOPSIS:
In 1950s Hollywood, movie star Guy Stone must marry a studio secretary in order to conceal his homosexuality. Sally has no idea her marriage is a sham, though, and turns Guy's life upside-down. Then he falls in love with a man.

Written and Directed by Richard Day
Produced by Andrew Trosmans and Michael Warwick
Released by SRO Pictures
in association with Here! Films
Genre: Comedy
Runtime: 96 Minutes

No, this is not a re-release of Joan Crawford's 1964 *Strait-Jacket*. This comedy/drama is called "Straight-Jacket," and in it the memory of gay actor Rock Hudson and the "glory" days of 1950s Hollywood live again.

Actor Matt Letscher is cast as Guy Stone, "America's Most Eligible Bachelor." His career is threatened when he's photographed leaving a gay bar. Tabloid headlines scream: HOMO STAR ARRESTED IN PERV PALACE.

Adam Greer and Matt Letscher

In the film, Guy's rapacious agent is acted brilliantly by Veronica Cartwright playing Jerry. She urges Guy into a loveless marriage with a ditzy secretary, who has the hots for Guy, not knowing he is homosexual.

Something of this nature actually happened to Rock Hudson, except his agent was Henry Willson, who virtually invented the casting couch. Rock Hudson was his chief money maker. Fearing exposure in *Confidential* magazine, Willson urged Rock to marry a secretary in the office.

After the marriage, Guy, in the film, complains that his wife is a "total bottom." In this new twist on the plot, Hudson – that is, Guy Stone – wants to keep his sexual preference a secret, of course, since it would destroy his career as a romantic leading man and prevent him from appearing in a remake of Ben-Hur. Another gay actor, Ramon Novarro, had filmed the silent screen version. He was later murdered by hustlers. In real life, the homophobic Charlton Heston got the lead role in the remake of Ben-Hur – not Rock Hudson.

The comedy heats up as the ditsy secretary, played by Carrie Preston, doesn't seem to realize what's going on. Guy falls for a handsome hunk named Rick Foster, as played by Adam Greer who looks good enough to eat.

If matters weren't complicated enough, Richard Day, the writer and director, tosses in a subplot with a McCarthy styled probe of alleged "Commies" – in this case, our hunks, Guy and Rick.

Based on an off-Broadway play, Straight-Jacket in filled with the camp humor gays love. For example, we love every moment that brought Guy's wisecracking valet, Victor (Michael Emerson) onto the screen. With deadpan delivery, he faces Guy who is complaining about no butter for his toast. "There hasn't been a stick of butter in the house since you dragged that trainee milkman upstairs."

Carrie Preston and Matt Letscher

Veronica Cartwright

Adam Greer

PRODUCTION CREW:

Director of Photography: Michael Pinky
Music: Stephen Edwards and Tom Erba
Editor: Chris Conlee
Production Designers: Kirsten McCarron and Mark Worthington
Costume Designer: Jim Hansen
Assistant Directors: Eric Fieland and Todd R. Schultz
Art Department: Christopher Isenegger, Johnny Knight, and Katherine LeBlond

WHAT THE CRITICS SAID:

"Desperate to certify his heterosexuality, Guy married his producer's secretary, Sally (Carrie Preston), a shrill blond bimbo who is not informed that she is being used as a smokescreen. Until his marriage, the air-headed Guy is a promiscuous rake, so in love with himself that on entering a gay bar he looks around and remarks, 'Who's the lucky winner tonight?'"

Stephen Holden *The New York Times*

"As Stone, Letscher looks and acts like the illegitimate playboy offspring of Ewan McGregor and Chris Isaak – slick and suave with impossibly wavy hair. After years of maintaining his lifestyle of discreet promiscuity with the help of his butler, Victor (the uproariously buttoned-down Michael Emerson), Stone's world starts to crumble as Sally invades his home with a little help from the Sears catalog. But most of all, Day's pyrotechnic dialogue and instinctive comic timing make *Straight-Jacket* a delight, especially when his actors unleash lines such as, "Without my fans, I'd be no better than they are," and Sally's description of love as a "Big, heart-shaped box full of chocolate razor blades." A talented craftsman of dark raillery, Day and his fixation on Hollywood melodrama are indulged to delicious effect in his sophomore effort."

Robert K. Elder *Chicago Tribune*

"*Straight-Jacket* gets easy laughs from Sally's clueless reactions to Guy's divinely splendid home furnishings – she simply replaces the more outrageous furniture and décor with items from Sears – but refrains from turning her into a mere object of ridicule. Indeed, pic takes pains to emphasize Guy's misgivings about the ruse. It helps a lot that Preston (repeating role she created in the 2000 off-Broadway production of *Straight-Jacket*) is sweetly engaged in her perky naïveté. But it helps even more that Letscher, who's smoothly persuasive and exceptionally funny during Guy's more selfish moments, is equally convincing when his evidences glimmers of empathy and decency."

Variety

CAST OF CHARACTERS

Matt Letscher (Guy Stone); Carrie Preston (Sally); Adam Greer (Rick Foster); Veronica Cartwright (Jerry); Victor Raider-Wexler (Saul); Jack Plotnick (Freddie Stevens); Michael Emerson (Victor)

WHAT THE CRITICS SAID (CONT'D):

"Richard Day's *Straight-Jacket* is a high camp take on a gay '50s movie star who marries to protect his image. The obvious inspiration is Rock Hudson, but this is no film *à clef*. Not only was Hudson's story different except for his brief marriage but he was also a shy, low-key and unpretentious man. Matt Letscher's Guy Stone is all arrogance, but amusingly self-knowingly so, and overflowing with the pride that inevitably goeth before a fall. *Straight-Jacket* has an abundance of delightfully bitchy dialogue and a serious sub-text, especially now that for gays that first decade of the 21st century is beginning to seem like a new dawn of the oppressive '50s."

Kevin Thomas *Los Angeles Times*

"Necco-colored sets and distractingly awful CGI long shorts almost mask the movie's real coup: Letscher's physique. A marvelously beefy, smoothly realized casing that actually looks like Hudson's or Kirk Douglas's, it basks in its natural abundance while displaying no modern anabolic ripples. His torso deserves its own title card. The gamest one here is Cartwright, emitting endless dignity despite flat in-jokes and being framed atop a toilet."

Edward Crouse *Village Voice*

"Guy has no trouble playing up his public persona by day and indulging his closeted, promiscuous real self at night ("What's the point in being famous if you can't use it to get laid?") But when a rival actor competing for the lead in *Ben-Hur* snaps some incriminating, potentially career-ruining photos, Guy is forced to marry a ditsy secretary (Carrie Preston) in a hurry and do his best to embrace the domestic life. Day, who adapted the movie from his own play, writes snappy one-liners that rival prime Paul Rudnick, and he gives the first half of the movie an appropriately snappy pace. The cast, which includes Veronica Cartwright as Guy's bossy agent and Michael Emerson as his hilariously dry butler, is game, too, helping to conceal the film's low-budget roots."

Rene Rodriguez *Miami Herald*

"The plan goes well enough until Guy falls in love with Rick (Adam Greer), the left-leaning screenwriter of his latest project, a drama about a coal miners union. Guy's newfound social conscience leads to a series of personal and professional complications in which he finds himself at the center of Hollywood's communist witch hunt."

Frank Scheck *Hollywood Reporter*

The Real Rock Hudson

Rock Hudson

Matt Letscher

Tarnation

Written and Directed by Jonathan Caouette
Produced by Jonathan Caouette
and Stephen Winter
Released by Wellspring Media
in association with American Vantage Media.
www.i-saw-tarnation.com
Genre: Documentary
Runtime: 88 Minutes

PLOT SYNOPSIS:
Made on a shoestring budget, this documentary tells the story of a gay boy growing up in red-state Houston and his trauma of dealing with a schizophrenic mother, whom he dearly loves. He survives a horrible, traumatic childhood, including abuse in foster homes. As a young boy Jonathan starts to record his life on video. Everything from Super-8 home movies to dramatic reenactments were used to create this harrowing story of a dysfunctional American family that takes on an aura of a B horror flick.

This extraordinary autobiographical documentary, both artful and intense, is the story of Jonathan Caouette, a 32-year-old gay Texan now living the life of a refugee from a red state in sophisticated New York with his boyfriend, David.

For the grand sum of $218.32, or so it is said, he created this film torn from the pages of his own life—or rather from film clips of his own life. Among the harrowing events, *Tarnation* depicts the pain of growing up with a schizophrenic mother.

David San Paz and Jonathan Caouette

Culled from 19 of the most painful years of his life, the home movie was created on a Macintosh and edited with the free iMovie software that came with the computer.

This dramatic reenactment of a dysfunctional Texas family was created using old answering machine messages, early short films, video diaries, and snippets of 80s pop culture songs, such as Glen Campbell's *Wichita Lineman*, everything beefed up by hundreds of stills and clips. The filmmaker's devotion to his mother comes through overwhelmingly in the frenetic, stroboscopic flickering of images.

The Boston Globe called the film "part time-capsule hot flash, part psychic collapse, part Faulkernian melodrama, part trash talk show, and all druggy fever dream conjured up with a lot of love."

A child model, Jonathan's mother fell off the roof of a Texas home. She was subjected to years of electroshock treatments and was repeatedly institutionalized. She ends up tragically damaged, her psyche in shattered pieces.

After abuse in foster homes and attempts at suicide, Jonathan is raised by his grandparents who don't have a clue. At the tender age of eleven, he is seen doing a precocious drag act. He also produces Super-8 slasher films with the kids in the neighborhood. His high school project is to stage a musical version of *Blue Velvet* with the cast lip-syncing Marianne Faithful songs.

At the age of ten, Jonathan arrives in Chicago, where he watches as his mother is raped.

Escaping from Texas, land of the George W. Bush clones, Jonathan arrives in New York. Fortunately he finds a stabilizing relationship with his boyfriend, David. Being gay doesn't destroy Jonathan's life: it seems to save it.

PRODUCTION CREW:

Director of Photography: Jonathan Caouette
Executive Producers: Vanessa Arteaga, Marie Therese Guirgis, John Cameron Mitchell, Gus Van Sant, and Ryan Werner
Music: John Califra and Max Avery Lichtenstein
Editors: Jonathan Caouette and Brian A. Kates

CAST OF CHARACTERS

Renee LeBlanc (Herself); Jonathan Caouette (Himself); Adolph Davis (Himself); Rosemary Davis (Herself); David San Paz (Himself); Michael Cox (Himself); Dagon James (Himself)

Jonathan Caouette and David San Paz   Jonathan Caouette

WHAT THE CRITICS SAID:

"*Tarnation* is its own resolution. Adrift in a selectively arranged saga of breakdowns, foster homes, abuse, attempted suicide, and brain damage, the artist clutches his camera as though it were a life raft, and apparently he survives. Caouette recalls thinking as a teenager that his story was a potential rock opera. Only time will tell, but *Tarnation* surely recounts an American life—grandiose fantasies amid pop detritus, success and celebrity distilled from a miasma of pain."

J. Hoberman *Village Voice*

"Jonathan Caouette's triumph over his harrowing childhood and adolescence is itself a huge accomplishment--but with *Tarnation* he has used art, wit, and a huge heart to forge his experiences into an unqualified masterpiece."

Lou Lumenick *New York Post*

"Looking at *Tarnation*, I wonder if the movie represents a new kind of documentary that is coming into being. Although home movies have been used in docs for decades, they were almost always, by definition, brief and inane. The advent of the video camera has meant that lives are recorded in greater length and depth than ever before; a film like *Capturing the Friedmans* (2003), with its harrowing portrait of sexual abuse and its behind-the-scenes footage of a family discussing its legal options, would have been impossible before the introduction of consumer video cameras. Jonathan Caouette not only experienced his life, but recorded his experience, and his footage of himself as a child says what he needs to say more eloquently than any actor could portray it or writer could describe it."

Roger Ebert

WHAT THE CRITICS SAID (CONT'D):

"Throughout the narrative, Jonathan refers to himself in the third person, a way of dramatizing the 'depersonalization disorder' that was either caused or permanently enhanced by smoking marijuana spiked with the lethal hallucinogen, PCP. Drugs, gay bars, the cinema (both popular and underground) and making home movies were his way of escape, his strategies for distancing himself from the terrible world."

Philip French *The Observer*

"Less a cheesy home video than a kaleidoscopic epic of the self, *Tarnation* is the 88-minute crystallization of the 20 years Caouette spent filming every corner of his life, principally his attempts to cope with his mother Renée's mental illness, which as a 30-year old, he's afraid might be lying inside waiting to take over his life."

Wesley Morris *The Boston Globe*

"You might call this knockout debut from Jonathan Caouette, 32, a documentary, since he put it together on a computer for $218 from home movies and other artifacts of growing up gay and living in Texas and New York with a mentally damaged mother. From age eleven, Caouette sidesteps trauma with musicals, horror flicks and pop-culture remnants that heal his psychic wounds. The result is a film that defines description. I'd call it some kind of miracle."

Peter Travers *Rolling Stone*

"Despite its avant-garde roots, *Tarnation* is always utterly absorbing and accessible, whether it's footage of an 11-year-old Caouette decked out in drag while hammily reciting an abused housewife's monologue that was clearly inspired by his mother, or scenes in which the grown up Caouette fulfills his lifelong fantasy of moving to New York, where he finds enough emotional stability in his relationship with his boyfriend David to gain perspective on his life. For all its disquieting moments—and there are many—*Tarnation* winds up being Caouette's adoring, big hearted ode to his mother. The movie may also be a work of catharsis, but it's also, unmistakably, an expression of love."

René Rodriguez *The Miami Herald*

"Getting so close to real life mental illness, via footage that spans many years renders *Tarnation* a uniquely potent experience. Caouette heightens that intensity by aping a sense of chaos and horror in editorial terms: split screen or densely layered images, frenetic cutting, color distortion, pop-culture touchstones (film and TV clips, etc), and audio tracks stacked to cacophonous effect."

Dennis Harvey *Variety*

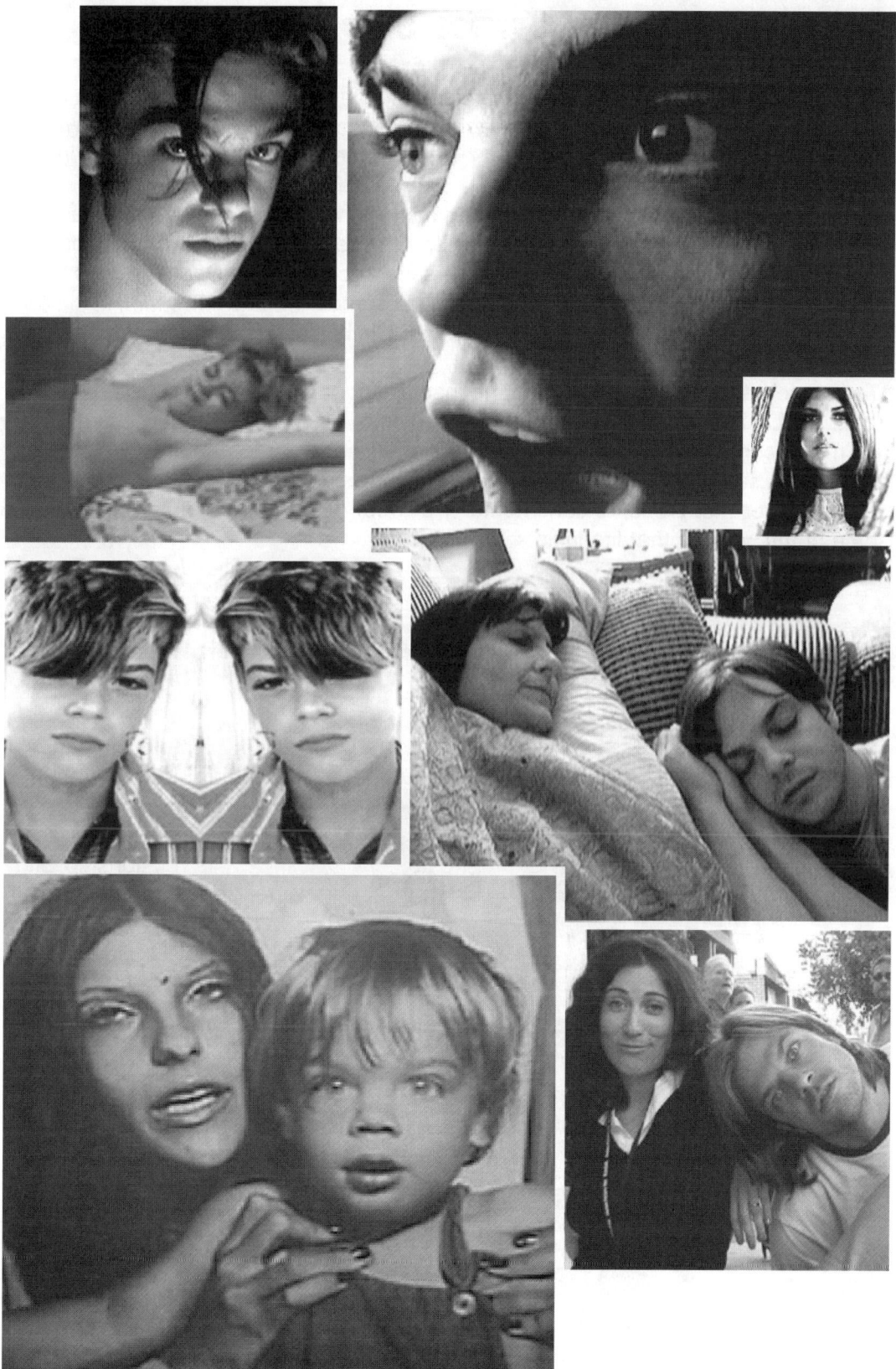

143

WHAT THE CRITICS SAID (CONT'D):

"This is nothing less than a one-of-a-kind film autobiography, a snapshot of a childhood hell from someone who used imagination and dreams to make it out alive."

Kenneth Turan *Los Angeles Times*

"Watching *Tarnation*, we're not just staring at a life; we're inside the emotional flow of Jonathan Caouette's memory system. The movie is a holy technological poem, a collage of suffering, a revelation, and perseverance in which Caouette tries to make sense of the torments that shaped his existence."

Owen Gleiberman *Entertainment Weekly*

"*Tarnation* is at once the record and the instrument of his survival. It tells a story about the costs of mental illness and denial, which is entwined with the story of a gay man's coming of age in suburban red-state America. More than anything else, though, this self portrait of an artist offers concrete support for the idea, usually treated, either with tiresome sentimentality or weary suspicion, that art can heal some of the wounds that life inflicts."

A.O. Scott *The New York Times*

Jonathan Caouette

144

Testosterone

Directed by David Moreton
and based on a novel
by James Robert Baker
(sharing screen-writing credits
with Dennis Hensley).
Released by Blue Streak Films
and Strand Releasing.
www.strandreleasing.com
Genre: Drama/Thriller
Runtime: 105 Minutes

PLOT SYNOPSIS:
The theme song of this movie might be, "Breaking up is hard to do." Lovers Dean and Pablo are a hot item until Pablo goes out for cigarettes and doesn't come back. Dean doesn't seem to know the motto of "move, on baby," so he follows his errant lover to Buenos Aires. And there the plot thickens in this convoluted adventure/thriller.

Let's face it: the reason many gay men (though far too few, according to box office receipts) went to see this film was all about publicity about *Über-hunk* and former Calvin Klein underwear model/actor, Antonio Sabato Jr., showing the full monty. At long last we know what he was keeping under wraps in those celebrated underwear ads that ended up on giant billboards on Times Square in New York and other cities.

The bad news is that you're allowed only a split second to see Antonio's jewels when they are surely deserving of at least five minutes of camera time…at least! The immediate question on everybody's lips who didn't see the film was this: "How big is it?"

Dario Dukah and Antonio Sabato Jr.

Put it this way, anybody in his right mind would hire him as a stripper, particularly at the now defunct Gaiety Theatre in New York where the dancers showed it hard. Antonio has a respectable package, certainly worthy of being photographed by the most expensive of cameras. As noted, the camera just didn't linger long enough for size queens in the theater to take accurate measurements.

Antonio is to be congratulated for dropping those drawers and treating us to what his fans really wanted to see. How many Hollywood hunks would dare to do that? Certainly not Leonardo DiCaprio. Cast as an Argentine sex-bomb, Antonio Sabato Jr. had a lot of balls to drop trou in front of camera.

Antonio told an interviewer for *The Advocate* that he was hoping *Testosterone* would jump start a stalled career. Regrettably, it doesn't seem to have done that. Such pity! He's one of the most charismatic actors in films today and could play any number of

Latin lover parts.

Of course, Antonio--certainly not his penis--is not the star of *Testosterone*. That honor goes to a less handsome, Canadian-born actor, David Sutcliffe, who plays Antonio's lover in the film. Antonio is cast as Pablo, David as Dean. David has the ongoing role of Rory's dad in the WB series, *The Gilmore Girls*. He's also starred in his own series, *I'm With Her*, for ABC.

Testosterone has plenty of hormones, and the guy-to-guy action is some of the hottest in any feature film. Dean plays a brilliant graphic novelist living with Pablo in a California beach house. Pablo goes out for a cigarette run and doesn't return. Ever the romantic, Dean blows his deadline and heads for Argentina where he learns that Pablo has retreated. The source of that information comes from Pablo's domineering mother (Sonia Braga) who detests her son's choice of lovers.

Arriving in Buenos Aires, one of the world's most decadent and photographable cities, Dean encounters one disaster after another in his search for "closure" with Pablo. In this intriguing locale, more evocative than Bogie's *Casablanca*, Dean soon learns that Pablo is the scion of a powerful local family. Sonia wants Dean out of town and will go to considerable lengths to accomplish her mission, sending scary cops and dangerous thugs after him.

In his search for Pablo, who no longer wants to be Dean's boyfriend, sexual situations unfold rapidly.

One reviewer likened *Testosterone* to a soft-core gay version of Robert Duvall's *Assassination Tango*. The far right would denounce this movie as obscene, but none of that crowd would ever go to see it any way, except closet queens in the Deep South renting it on DVD.

Although Pablo is the love of his life, Dean picks up a handsome Argentine hunk in a bookstore. A piece of hot stuff named Marcos is played by Leonardo Brzezicki, who, it turns out, was Pablo's former lover. One of the hottest scenes in the film occurs not

Antonio Sabato: On Taking Risks

For the Italian-born, Spanish-speaking Sabato, working in Argentina felt, in a way, like going home again. "The people are just open with all their hearts," he says. "I'll definitely be going back there." The project also offered the actor a welcome break from the more bureaucratic worlds of studio films and network television. "There aren't any agents calling you down there because it's too far away," he says with a laugh. "In Hollywood, sometimes they put you in a box and they want you to be a certain way. But as an actor you want to express yourself in different ways. *Testosterone* is kind of saying 'We're taking a risk here and there's nothing you can do about it.' Hopefully, it will allow me to open up some doors and show that I am fearless in my work."

146

between Dean and Marco, but between Marco and another handsome Argentine hunk Guillermo, as played by Dario Dukah. Incidentally, if you don't like handsome Latino hunks, stay away from this sexy flicker.

At one point, Dean watches like a voyeur through a cracked mirror opening into a linen closet at the seedy and misnamed Ritz Hotel. There he sees Guillermo and Marco getting it on Argentine style. As one reviewer so accurately put it, *Testosterone* is a "movie for connoisseurs of male eye candy."

The man eater in the film is also mentioned Sonia Braga, who, as Pablo's mother, is the ultimate Latino bitch. She's actually Brazilian, not from Argentina, but what does that matter? She's an international pussy from hell, a gay man's worst nightmare to have as a "mother-in-law."

The second actor delivering the strongest and most vivid role is Jennifer Elise Cox, who plays Dean's tarantula agent. She's virtually the comedy relief in this film, depicting an agent so voracious that she even promises "to shave my pussy for you."

Down in Buenos Aires--no jokes are made about whorish Evita--Dean discovers a beautiful cafe owner, Sofia, brilliantly played by Celina Font, who has more sensitivity and subtlety than all the other actors in the film.

A lot of the action that unfolds in Argentina is undefined and confusing, although the earlier scenes depicting Los Angeles are straightforward and more understandable. Chances are, you'll remain fascinated as Dean charges a machete to his credit card and takes off for that final confrontation with the wandering Pablo.

In this obsessive love story, director Moreton has discovered a more intriguing terra firma than he did in his 1999 queen teen tract, *Edge of Seventeen*.

David Sutcliffe

Antonio Sabato Jr.

Jennifer Coolidge

Leaving a theater after seeing *Testosterone* in New York, one movie-goer was commenting on the film to his lover. We eavesdropped. "I don't blame that Dean character. I would follow Antonio Sabato to the ends of the earth just for one night with him."

PRODUCTION CREW:

Director of Photography: Ken Kelsch
Music: Marco D'Ambrosio
Editors: Mallory Gottlieb and Roger Schulte
Production Designer: Jorge Ferrari

WHAT THE CRITICS SAID:

"The director does provide a gratuitious nude shot of Sabato that demonstrates that his years as a Calvin Klein underwear model were well deserved."

Frank Scheck *The Hollywood Reporter*

"Surprise after surprise follows in this increasingly dark comedy, which is loaded with sharp observations and exceptionally complex characterizations that are often the mark of a skilled adaptation of a novel. In this instance, director David Moreton, who made his mark with the memorable *Edge of Seventeen*, co-adapted, with Dennis Hensley, a James Robert Baker novel, and the result is a confident, shrewd comedy, at once sexy and gleefully nasty."

Kevin Thomas *Los Angeles Times*

"True to its title, the film traffics in enough hot guys and sexy action to tap the gay market, especially as a DVD release."

David Rooney *Variety*

CAST OF CHARACTERS

David Sutcliffe (Dean Seagrave); Celina Font (Sofia); Antonio Sabato Jr. (Pablo Alesandro); Jennifer Coolidge (Louise); Leonardo Brzezicki (Marcos); Sonia Braga (Pablo's mother); Dario Dukah (Guillermo); Jennifer Elise Cox (Sharon, the Perky Chick); Davenia McFadden (Marnie); Ezequiel Abeijón (Rogelio)

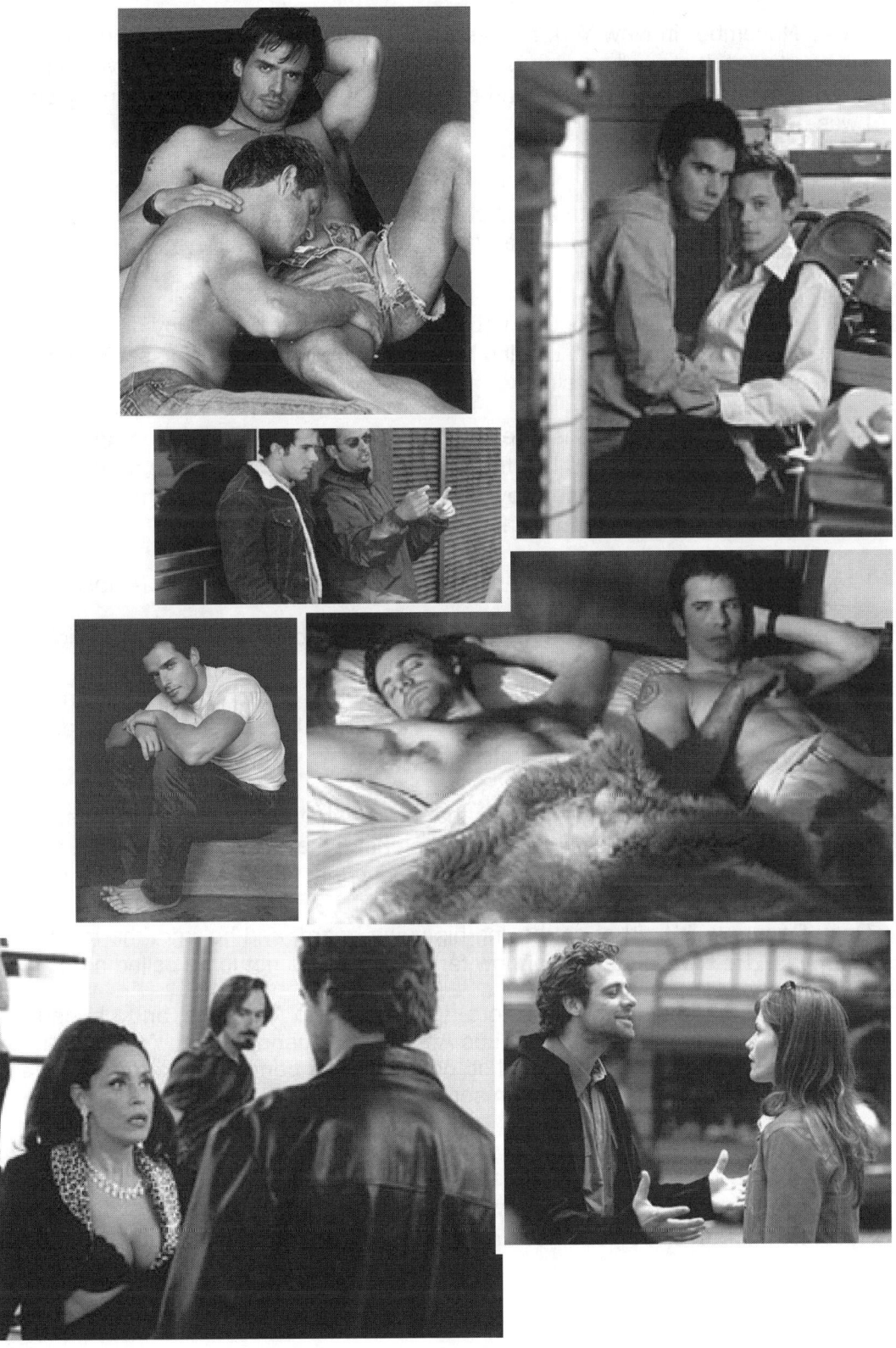

Director's Statement

It was November in New York and as I walked down Greenwich Avenue toward my apartment. It started pouring rain. Not just a friendly sprinkle. Not even a seasonal shower. But a full-on cats-and-dogs kind of thing. But luck was on my side; I was near a bookstore.

I ducked in and began acting like I had been on my way to the bookstore all along. I sauntered around a bit, and then picked up a book in the "new releases" section. *Testosterone* it was called. I flipped open the front cover and began reading the description.

This novel seemed to be about an obsessive love affair. Some guy named Dean was going on a frenzied quest to find his missing Latin lover Pablo...seeking truth, vengeance, and, yes, even closure.

And the cherry on top of this already literary cake? The final paragraph of the book's jacket synopsis goes like this: The problem is, Dean might be crazy. Or everyone might be lying. Either way, Dean has a machete--because the chainsaw was too loud--and he's just found Pablo.

I bought the book immediately. So began my four-year journey with *Testosterone*.

Testosterone is about what happens when you don't take a man seriously. Everyone underestimates Dean. His boyfriend walks out on him without a word. A middle-aged woman doesn't flinch when he pulls a gun on her, and another woman laughs in his face, saying to him, "Fags don't kill." Dean is frustrated, and he channels that frustration into hatred that fuels his vengeance.

From the beginning nobody imagines that he is able to carry out his threats. Gay men are often seen as artistic, but not threatening; they are fun to have at a party, even better as your decorator, but not needed when it comes to battle plans.

Dean Seagrave is tired of not having his voice heard, and he's got the machete to prove it. He's walking proof of how far a man will go not to be called a pussy.

A year after that day in the bookstore, I took a trip to Argentina, and I began to consider relocating the story from Los Angeles to Buenos Aires. Argentina is a tradition-bound Latin culture, and it provides the perfect backdrop for man wrestling with issues of being taken seriously.

In Buenos Aires Dean's self-involvement isolates him in a culture where he doesn't speak the language nor understand society's norms. He lands in a web of intrigue, and easily becomes a pawn for those with more strategic plans. In his quest to find Pablo, Dean comes dangerously close to losing himself.

A Thousand Clouds of Peace...

(Mil nubes de paz...)

Written and Directed by Julián Hernández.
Produced by Robert Fiesco.
Released by Nubes Cine
in association with Strand Releasing.
www.strandrel.com
Genre: Drama/Romance
Runtime: 80 Minutes
Spanish with English subtitles

PLOT SYNOPSIS:
Seventeen-year-old Gerardo and his friend Bruno have split up. Gerardo finds himself wandering aimlessly about the streets of Mexico City. As he meanders, he is tortured by images: every male body he sees rekindles memories of his love, who is with him once again in his imagination. However, his wet dreams do not alleviate his suffering, nor does masturbation provide him with any kind of relief. Even his brief, surprising sexual encounters with strangers can't help him get over the pain of his loss. Gerardo constructs a tower of loneliness in which he may preserve his desire for Bruno from the onslaught of the real world. He is holding onto the fantasy images of his erstwhile love in an endless farewell, in a vast, endless city.

Its plot is simple to the point of being banal, and its deadpan and its lack of artifice might make you search for deeper meaning than what is actually here. The visuals are shadowy, the characters rather inexplicably suffer sometimes agonizing pain in something approaching mute despair, and you can't help but compare the characters, and their suffering, to mange-eaten beasts of burden living their lives in an emotional vacuum.

Manuel Grapain Zaquelarez and Juan Carlos Ortuño

An ode to adolescent pain and the undeserving ex-boyfriend who got away, it has virtually no dialogue of note, no success at fleshing out characters and their motivations, and absolutely not a shred of humor. As portrayed by Gerardo, who's about as glum and melancholy as a teenager can possibly be, the scenario of unrequited love on the backstreets of Mexico City is bleak indeed. Before the end of the film, you almost wish that the Mexican Division of Tourism had gotten hold of it, permeated with music and color, and added their input to city scenes that make even good neighborhoods of Mexico City look like a lunar landscape in an existential freeze.

In the words of Stephen Holden, writing for *The New York Times*, "The movie, handsomely photographed by Diego Arizmendi, leaves you grasping at straws about who Gerardo (the central character) is. Like Gerardo, the movie is content to wallow in an adolescent obsession that's as vague as its title.

Gerardo is an absolute flop at expressing himself, although he's good at mutely channeling oceans of pain to the audience at large. Alas, actor Juan Carlos Ortuño isn't experienced enough to handle what, in the hands of a better actor, might have become a volcanic portrait of repressed pain and rage. He has a lot of sex (the director here was not afraid of frontal nudity) but he isn't particularly adept at hustling, getting conflicted every time a john, even one who's a potential boyfriend, tries to give him money to assuage his own guilt. (In some cases, johns give him money just as a means of having him go away.) It's all rather self-consciously arty, very black-and-white, very emotionally blank, and very slow. Some critics kindly compare the film to a work by Michelangelo Antonioni: In the words of Stephen Murray, a writer for *Epinions*, "Perhaps this film's budget was too low to include anyone writing dialogue, though the look of chic alienation seems to draw on the precedent of Michelangelo Antonioni, a director not much interested in dialogue, and very interested in photographing things, including expressionless and mute human objects in industrial wastelands."

Perhaps the premises of this film are flawed. Is Gerardo completely crazy, or just a lost teen who revels in his romantic angst? He is abandoned early in the film by his closeted, once-upon-a-time boyfriend, the dashing and strikingly handsome Bruno, who doesn't seem like such a bad chap.

Gerardo draws comfort from the text of a letter, written by a stranger, which he finds in the garbage. *Latino fantaisie*? A Mexican version of Miss Haversham mourning, in ways that are more than a bit psychotic, the end of a *grand amour*? Drab, inarticulate, and colorless, the film quickly evolves into a dark and brooding coming-of-age story that takes a quick turn to despair. There's a hopeless kind of existentialist despair, a Spanish-speaking version of *No Exit* written all over this film. We compare it to a dog-eared Mexican replay of a *bête noir* film, but in this case a *bête noir* that might have been inspired by a particularly embittered French existentialist in postwar Europe.

By the end of the film, Gerardo has constructed a tower of loneliness in which he preserves romantic fantasies of his long-departed love within the gray and brooding confines ("an impenetrable, blank-faced melancholy" as phrased by Stephen Holden) of an enormous and anonymous city. The film has an appealing amount of gratuitous, anonymous sex instead of comic relief.

Perhaps this film is best interpreted as a bravely honest vehicle for the accurate portrayal of the despair of Mexican youth facing the social Nothingness of the post-millennium. With huge respect for all parties concerned, if life for teens in Mexico City is as unfulfilling as what's depicted in this film, and if I were 17 and prowling for whatever reason through the garbage dumps of that city, I'd maneuver and manipulate my way across the Rio Grande too.

What's in a name?

The name of this film might be more intriguing than the film itself. Everything about it communicates its wish to be as arty as possible, and after viewing the film, one wonders if the cheerfully optimistic title wasn't hard-wired to the final product merely as a means of making it less depressing. The full Spanish-language title is *Mil nubes de paz cercan el cielo, amor, jamás acabarrás de ser amor*. Creatively translated, that means, "A Thousand Clouds of Peace Fence the Sky, [my] Love; You Will Always Be [the One I] Love; Never Will Cease You Being Love [for me]. Regrettably, the title of the film is the only poetically effusive thing in the entire film. Everything else is gray, cheerless, mute/inarticulate, and so depressing as to leave its audience feeling merely numb.

PRODUCTION CREW:

Director of Photography: Diego Arizmendi
Producer: Robert Fiesco
Editors: Emiliano Arenales Osorio and Jacopo Hernández
Production Designer: Carolina Jiménez
Sound: Aurora Ojedo and Enrique L. Rendón Jaramillo

CAST OF CHARACTERS

Salvador Alvarez (Susana); Gloria Andrade (Girl); Llane Fragoso (Mirella); Martha Gómez (Martha); Rosa María Gómez (Mary); Manuel Grapain Zaquelarez (Jorge); Marcos Hernández (Antonio); Perla De La Rosa (Anna); Miguel Loaiza (Adrián); Pablo Molina (Andrés); Mario Oliver (Umberto); Juan Carlos Ortuño (Gerardo); Clarissa Rendón (Nadia); Pilar Ruíz (Lola); Martin Solís (Boy); Juan Carlos Torres (Bruno)

Manuel Grapain Zaquelarez   Juan Carlos Ortuño   Manuel Grapain Zaquelarez
and Juan Carlos Ortuño

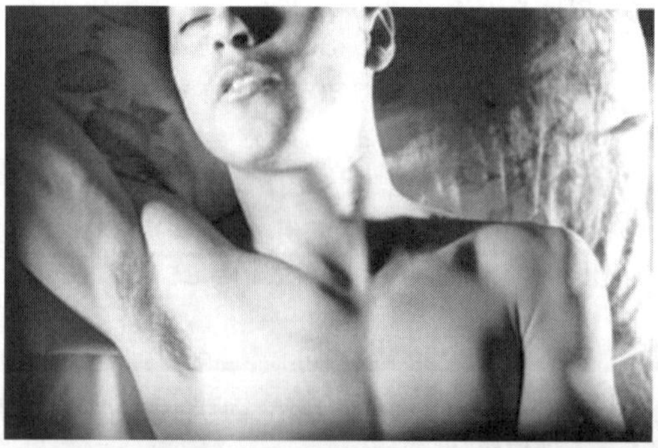

154

WHAT THE CRITICS SAID:

"The focus of this black-and-white film, directed by Julián Hernández, is a romanti-cally obsessed 17-year-old boy, Gerardo (Juan Carlos Ortuño), living on the streets of Mexico City. Gerardo, who has dropped out of school and spends most of his time sulking on a bridge where men cruise one another for sex, pines for Bruno (Juan Carlos Torres), who leaves him at the beginning of the film. But for all the specifics that are given, Bruno might as well not exist.

The movie is a bleak, static mood piece about adolescent emptiness. There's little dialogue, and what there is offers the scantest information about Gerardo, who, as played by Mr. Ontuño, conveys an impenetrable blank-faced melancholy. Gerardo has unsatisfying sex with strangers, but these intimacies only remind him of what he lacks. One man tempts him into sex, then beats him up. Gerardo finds an anony-mous love letter in the trash and takes its words to heart, even though it was written for someone else."

Stephen Holden *New York Times*

"The title of Julián Hernández's first feature film provides fair warning that it aspires to be an "art film. "A Thousand Clouds of Peace" is less than transparent, but get the full title: "Mil nubes de paz cercan el cielo, amor, jamás acabarás de ser amor"! Translating it into English, I'd add possessive pronouns, and render this as "A Thousand Clouds of Peace Fence the Sky, [My] Love; You Will Always Be [the One I] Love (a more word-for-word translation is "A Thousand Clouds of Peace Fence the Sky, Love; Never Will Cease You Being Love [for me]. This, um, shall we say "poet-ic" effusion is directed by the buzz-cut seventeen-year-old Gerardo (Juan Carlos Ortuño) as Bruno (Juan Carlos Torres), the man who has broken with Gerardo, bro-ken his heart, and imprinted himself forever as the love of Gerardo's life (that is, for Gerardo, Bruno is Love itself).

The movie really is about a love-struck adolescent, but the title is misleading in that he is nearly mute and not at all given to poetic ejaculations (he traffics in more mun-dane ones, although he is looking for love more than seeking payment in his many sexual encounters, and is sometimes given money as a dismissal by men he hoped were potential lovers)."

Stephen Murray *Epinions.com*

WHAT THE CRITICS SAID (CONT'D):

"Although the title *A Thousand Clouds of Peace Fence the Sky; Love: Your Being Loved Will Never End* suggests a euphoric, pleasant story, in fact Mexican director Julián Hernández presents a noir film in black and white. The title is from a poem by Pier Paolo Pasolini. Whereas John Rechy describes angst among reasonably mature gays in his *City of Night* (1963), the movie *A Thousand Clouds of Peace* focuses on Gerardo (played by Juan Carlos Ortuño), a seventeen-year-old hustler who tried desperately to find male companionship in the daytime. Gerardo evidently was reared by a single mother (played by Perla De La Rosa) whom he left to ply his trade; he never graduated from high school, so he has no other marketable skill, though he has a part-time job at a pool hall, where he meets some of his johns. When the film begins, he is providing oral sex in an automobile alongside a road near his residence."

Political Film Society

"Nothing but a groundbreaking masterpiece in Mexican cinema. Hernández has created a haunting and subtle fable about the eternal nature of love."

Bruno Benton

"In *A Thousand Clouds of Peace*, writer-director Julian Hernandez has a unique point of view and a keen eye for composition, and that is too often not the case when it comes to most films.

Perhaps that's why this bleak portrait of a 17-year-old boy recovering from a painful breakup won the Teddy Award for the best lesbian/gay film at last year's Berlin Film Festival, and was nominated for seven Mexican Oscars.

But the fact remains that Hernández's debut feature is a thuddingly slow, often wordless portrait of emotional pain – a legitimate approach to the material, to be sure, but not when that emotion is filtered through a young, inexperienced actor who has about as much expression as a zombie in *Dawn of the Dead*."

G. Allen Johnson *San Francisco Chronicle*

Touch of Pink

Written and directed by Ian Iqbal Rashid.
Released by Sony Pictures Classics and Martin
Pope Productions.
www.sonyclassics.com
Genre: Drama/Comedy/Romance
Runtime: 92 Minutes

PLOT SYNOPSIS:
Alim is an Ismaili Canadian who lives in London, thousands of miles from his family, for one very good reason--he has a boyfriend. His ideal gay life begins to unravel when his mother shows up to find him a proper Muslim girlfriend and demands that he return to Canada for his cousin's extravagant wedding.
--Sujit R. Varma

The most obvious theme of *Touch of Pink* revolves around a "coming out" conflict, but the larger theme pushes much further. Not only has the hero hidden his sexual identity from his mother; he's virtually divorced himself from his family's South Asian culture as well. Within the depiction of a subculture (gay identities becoming identified and defined) within another subculture (a community of Ismaelian Muslims living in Toronto), the film emphasizes the need for people to live comfortably with who they most naturally are.

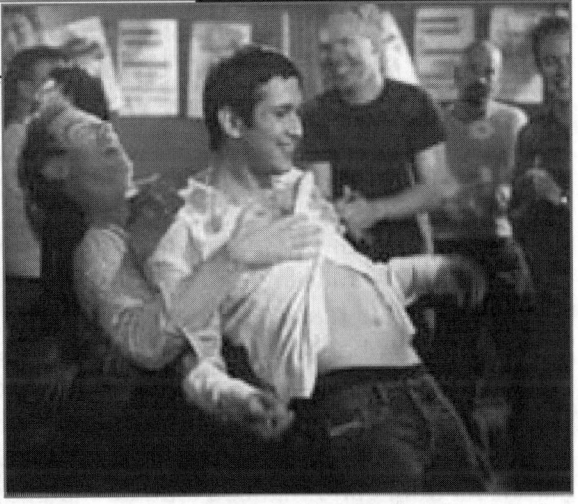

Kristen Holden-Reid
and Jimi Mistry

The movie contains some of the elements of an old-fashioned screwball comedy, with quaint references to the spirit of a reincarnated Cary Grant. Cheerful and chipper, with a kind of retro charm that's re-created by *Sex in the City's* Kyle MacLaughlin, he lives within the hero, unbeknownst even to the hero's lover, Giles, as the kind of secret and imaginary friend that lonely children adopt for company.

As the film deepens, *Touch of Pink* explores the way its characters come out of their sexual and cultural closets, learning to love who they are and where they came from, culturally. In the words of one of its co-producers, "it deals with characters that are ultimately required to be true to themselves even though they are slightly out of step with the rest of the world around them."

As played by Jimi Mistry, Alim is a young, sexy, South-Asian Canadian who's living in London, working as a still photographer in the movie business, and trying, with the help of his imaginary reincarnation of Cary Grant, to live up to the glamorous standards of old Hollywood. Playing Alim's partner, actor Kristen Holden-Reid is a handsome English economist who's charming, intelligent, and comfortable with who he is. Nuru (Alim's mother), acted by Sue Mathew, arrives in London for a visit from her home in Toronto, hoping to pull Alim into the orbit of the Ismaelian community, where, she hopes, he'll find a Muslim bride, raise a family, and "do his duty."

Nuru, it's revealed during the progression of the film, had suffered a nervous break-down after the death of her husband several years after Alim's birth, and left the care of her only child to a conservative aunt back in Toronto before moving to London to test her mettle in the big city. It is during that period, we learn, that the young Alim developed a secret dependency on his "imaginary friend," smooth and unflappable "Cary Grant."

Alas, Nuru's experience in London in the 1960s did not evolve into the whirlwind of romance that she had hoped it would be. ("I imagined myself as Doris Day from movies we had seen back in Kenya, but not surprisingly, no one wanted an Indian version of Doris Day.") Now, reappearing on the London scene after years of absence, her old memories, and old humiliations, are re-awakened, and her judgments about the

---

Invoking the Spirit of Cary Grant

Viewers of *Touch of Pink* need, early in the film, to accept the premise that Alim, the handsome Muslim hero, is constantly accompanied by a spirit version of Cary Grant. Created many years previously by a lonely adolescent as a barrier against having been abandoned by his mother, the "guiding spirit" continues to motivate and guide Alim through the obstacle course of the conflicting cultures that is his life.

According to director Ian Iqbal Rashid, "Cary Grant gave such silky, seamless, and transcendent performances that, as much as he was an actor, Cary Grant became a state of mind. When invoking a cultural icon, however, in the form of a modern-day theatrical performance, one must tread carefully. We needed an actor who'd do more than just an impersonation. The thing to keep in mind is that the Cary Grant in the film is actually a creation of Alim's, an emanation of his psyche, so we could take a few liberties. The actor really had to nail the characterization without becoming a caricature himself. Anything too cheesy would negatively affect our view of Alim. We finally selected Kyle MacLaughlan, both because he liked the role and because he had the elegance, wit, and slightly period handsomeness that the character required."

"I'm not playing Cary Grant, exactly," says MacLaughlan. "I'm doing a generation or two removed from Cary Grant. I represent to Alim certain qualities he feels are important. Qualities like the abilty to handle himself in any situation. Alim, before the end of the film, comes to realize that he doesn't need to rely on me for those qualities: He has them in himself, which is something that I've been telling him throughout the course of the film."

lifestyle of her son (whom she still doesn't realize is gay) become more shrill.

Enter Giles, a laudably diplomatic lover, who makes endearing efforts to take Nuru out for a day of sightseeing and shopping in London. Unexpectedly, Nuru grows fond of Giles. Giles even shows promise of being the kind of man that Nuru would have liked to have met all those years before.

Alas, Giles can't be Nuru's Hollywood ending, as a jealous Alim makes clear when he finally comes out to his mother. Giles, ever the diplomat, is horrified by Alim's behavior, and walks out. Nuru, devastated, returns home to Toronto. Only Cary is on hand to help Alim forge a plan of action. Cary, fearing that Alim is slipping away (in this film, even the ghosts have feelings) cheerfully tries to "Indianize" himself, donning a safari costume and babbling on about *Gunga Din* and the conquest of the subcontinent.

The ending is happy, as lovers Giles and Alim reunite. Nuru and Alim reach a shared sense of honesty and affection and Nuru moves into a deeper appreciation of her own role as a sophisticated and free-thinking international woman, perhaps (as the plot line hints) with an upcoming new romance of her own.

Jimi Mistry, Sue Mathew, and Kristen Holden-Reid

Kristen Holden-Reid
and Jimmy Mistry

Kyle MacLachlan and Jimi Mistry

WHAT THE CRITICS SAID:

"The title of *Touch of Pink*, a clever and big-hearted gay screwball comedy, has a triple meaning--most obviously, its reference to the Cary Grant/Doris Day romantic comedy, *A Touch of Mink*. It also refers to an Anglo's skin color--and to the sexual preferences of Alim, an Indian-Canadian film-set photographer who shares a flat in London with his hunky and devoted economist boyfriend, Giles."

Lou Lumenick *New York Post*

"Rashid's optimistic fairy tale is inventive, in a show-queen way, when it references Grant's films, including the 1962 Grant-and-Doris Day comedy, *That Touch of Mink*."

Lisa Schwarzbaum *Entertainment Weekly*

"*Touch of Pink* is lovely and often comical, with Rashid poking affectionate fun at his exuberantly *nouveau riche*--and sometimes hypocritical Toronto relatives. By the time the film is over, it has also become a deft comment on how potent the movies are in shaping our values and expectations. *Touch of Pink* pays homage to classic screwball comedy yet never confuses it with real life."

Kevin Thomas *Los Angeles Times*

"In *Touch of Pink*, Kyle MacLachlan does an uncanny impersonation of Cary Grant as a sort of fairy godmother to an extremely stress-prone gay guy. MacLachlan is playing the Grant from the urbane late period of *Charade* and *North by Northwest*, and he turns Grant's mellifluous bellow into something haltingly phonetic and prissy, but it still seems right: He's nothing like Grant, yet exactly as he appeared to be."

Wesley Morris *Boston Globe*

"The only real touch of class in *Touch of Pink*, a rickety little romantic comedy whose title riffs on the 1962 movie *That Touch of Mink*, is Kyle MacLachlan's dead-on impersonation of Cary Grant. Lounging around in a paisley dressing gown, dropping pallid witticisms in Grant's signature staccato style with just the right accent, Mr. MacLachlan finds an easy balance between affectionate imitation and amusing parody."

Stephen Holden *The New York Times*

CAST OF CHARACTERS

Jimi Mistry (Alim); Kyle MacLachlan (Spirit of Cary Grant); Sue Mathew (Nuru); Kristen Holden-Reid (Giles); Brian George (Hassan); Veena Sood (Dolly); Raoul Bhaneja (Khaled); Lisa Repo-Martell (Delia); Andrew Gillies (Raymond); Quancetia Hamilton (Airplane Woman); Dean McDermott (Alisdair Keith); Barna Moricz (Alex); Sam Moses (Vendor); Sanjay Talwar (Karim); Linda Thorson (Giles' Mother)

The Real Cary Grant

Cary Grant

Kyle MacLaghlan

Ian Iqbal Rashid on Indian vs. Western Cinema

"Cinema plays a huge part in the lives of people in and from the sub-continent. Those of us who have migrated to the West have carried that love of cinema with us. However, there's a tight-rope walk between assimilating into Western culture, and yet keeping a sense of who you are. The process of assimilation can erase aspects of identity, both cultural and personal, which are special and unique. Yet, it's very seductive to become part of a dominant culture, to belong to the home team-and *Touch of Pink* is about that as well."

PRODUCTION CREW:

Director of Photography: David A. Makin
Executive Producer: Charlotte Mickie
Associate Producers: Brent Barclay and Andrea Glinski
Editor: Susan Maggi
Production Designer: Gavin Mitchell
Composer: Andrew Lockington
Costume Designer: Joyce Schure

Transfixed
(Mauvais genres)

Directed by Francis Girod and written by
Francis Girod and Phillip Cougrand.
Based on the novel by Brigitte Aubert.
Produced by Humbert Balsan, with Marie-Astrid
Lamboray as executive producer.
Released by Picture This! Entertainment.
www.picturethisent.com/minisites/transfixed
Genre: Crime Thriller
Runtime: 106 Minutes
French with English subtitles

PLOT SYNOPSIS:
In this thriller, Bo is a trans-sexual prostitute in Brussels who left home after being abused by her father. It's rare in that the star of this film is a trans-gendered character. As the plot develops, a series of grisly murders within the city's sexual fringe are inextricably linked to Bo. This detective mystery is replete with unexpected ironies and plot twists.

Robinson Stévenin and
Richard Bohringer

Filmed for the most part in Brussels, and originally intended as a Franco-Belgian made-for-TV movie, *Transfixed* is an intelligent, absorbing, and very European film about life on the GLBT fringe. Its main focus is on a series of grisly murders inflicted upon members of the cross-dressing, sometimes transsexual fringe of Brussels' nightlife and prostitution scene.

En route, it transmits some subtle but driving social commentaries about class and educational differences within Belgian society, and--in a way that only a completely uninhibited drag queen can do--it manages to drive home some telling truths about sexual hypocrisy among the bourgeoisie.

Above all, however, it's a film about prostitutes and drag queens, how and why some of them got to be that way, the compromises some of them maintain to survive, and the enormous courage it takes for many of them to carry on, safely and without harassment, throughout the course of their day-to day-lives.

The viewer is left with the disturbing realization that it isn't particularly safe to be an out-and-proud drag queen on the sexual edge. Before the film's end, everyone is suspect of the darkest motives, and the viewer is immersed in a shadowy state of psychological torment wherein absolutely no one, including the police, can be trusted.

In many ways, *Transfixed* evokes the *film noir* neuroses of the best of its genre, earning empathy for characters (cross-dressing prostitutes) who have, in the past, only rarely been singled out for the cinematic spotlight.

It opens with a scene wherein Badouin ("Bo") Ancellin, the waif-like protagonist, stylishly dressed in what might be Chanel, returns to pay a visit to his *haute-bourgeoise* grandmother, now living in a nursing home, but still recognizable as a sensitive woman well-trained in the social graces. A few moments before, Grandmamma had not recognized her son (who, it is later established, seemed keen on brutalizing Bo during his formative years) even when the police lead him away in handcuffs on suspicion of pedophilia.

In a bizarre twist, Grandmamma mistakes her extremely stylish crossdressing grandson (Badouin) for his mother (her daughter-in-law), Elsa. Granted, most grandsons might opt not to cross-dress during visits to their grannies in a nursing home, but even so, Bo has troubles, it appears, being understood within his family unit.

It's established early that Badouin has a spine made of steel, something he'll need as he's thrust into the vortex of what quickly develops into a full-scale police search for a demented serial murderer who enjoys carving up the nubile bodies from Brussels' community of cross-dressing entertainers. It's also established that Bo is both well-mannered and well-educated, speaking in an almost involuntary upper-class diction even when surrounded by the klieg lights of the Brussels police force, some of whom come across as demented, and possibly sexually perverted, lower-class thugs.

Throughout the film, Badouin does the art of cross-dressing proud. He's tough yet vulnerable, and he dresses with undeniable panache. (*Drag Queen Alert*: his fashion sense is subtle, stylish, and European. Viewers quickly accept his fashion priorities, probably because his humanity and vulnerability come roaring through.) He's at his most engaging when, flush with the victory of a coquettish conquest, say, on Johnny, the brooding and sadistic object of his love and affection, he exudes a kind of feminine/macho swagger.

The role is skillfully and subtly played by actor Robinson Stévenin, whose looks were

Director Francis Girod on gore and violence

The flim also presents us with a serial killer. How did you deal with the problem of showing violence?

Francis Girod: "*Transfixed* is not a film with a lot of gore. The murders are shown in an elliptical, stylized manner and treated without voyeurism of any kind. What interested me in the character of the serial killer was his story. Johnny, like Bo, had a miserable childhood, and he found release in murder, which enabled him to resolve his sexual problems. He is a child who witnessed a primal murder and who cannot stop reproducing the primitive scene. Between the young transvestite and the serial killer there exists a form of mutual recognition that generates a phenomenon of attraction/repulsion between the two young men. We witness muders in *Transfixed*, but there is no need to make a big deal out of it! I wouldn't describe this as a novel by Madame de la Fayette, but it is, first and foremost, a love story."

described by film critic Duncan Pittman as "a strange mélange of boyish charm and classic feminine glamour--think Jeanne Moreau meets Audrey Hepburn." Bo's would-be boyfriend is a brooding stud named (as in the Piaf song), Johnny (Stéphane Metzger), who responds to Bo's affection with calculating and sadistic cruelty. Johnny makes a living messing around in threesomes with other sadists and with decadent heiresses on the far side of middle age. Nonetheless, Badouin adores Johnny without reservation (after all, this film was partially conceived in France), getting humiliated and bludgeoned as part of the romance. And love hurts, especially as we're made to see that Johnny is the whodunit who, except for luck and the evasive skill of the street-smart Bo, would almost certainly have carved up Bo as his next victim.

Robinson Stévenin won a César Award, the French Oscar-equivalent, for his role as the transsexual Bo. His cohort, actor Richard Bohringer, who plays the cynical and sometimes menacing Detective Huysmans, is a two-time winner of the César award. Bohringer's handsome and craggy face, and engaging French-thug style, are widely recognized throughout Europe and the French-speaking world.

Who is our favorite character, after Bo, in the film?: It's Maeva, played by William Nadylam. The strapping and muscular drag queen is depicted with a get-down and get-dramatic persona. Sadly, she becomes a victim of the serial killer, but the audience gets a kind of cathartic surprise when the scary-looking stranger who appears to have been stalking Bo/Badouin turns out to be Maeva's aimiable and charming son, conceived back when Maeva was bumping real-time pussy, trawling on the other side of the gender-related fence.

Robinson Stévenin and Stéphane Metzger

Robinson Stévenin

Richard Bohringer

PRODUCTION CREW:

Director of Photography: Thierry Jault
Music: Alexandre Desplat
Editor: Isabelle Dedieu
Sound Editor: Christophe Winding
Production Designer: Perrine Rulens

Brussels: Pedophile fathers & sexual deviants

The Belgian capital, thanks partly to its role as the centerpiece of the United Europe, has come a long way since the days when its neighbors to the south, especially France, dismissed it as a boring and hidebound backwater, a "whited sepulcher" as described by Joseph Conrad. Is there more in the Belgian capital than waffles, bureaucracies, and the mannequin piss? Here's an insight or two directly from the mouth of the film's director, Francis Girod.

"I don't consider Belgium a country of pedophile fathers and sexual deviants. Recent events have shown that, in this regard, France can hold its own with Belgium! No, I wanted to shoot in Belgium because I spent my adolescence in Brussels. It's a city that I like very much and it seems to me that it has an ambience that lends itself well to a somewhat fantastic detective story plot. In Brussels, a city that, for economic reasons, has been subject to chaotic architectural transformations, I found locations that were perfect for the film: dark, paved streets that recall Jack the Ripper and large lofts located in brick buildings that are reminiscent of New York. I also had the pleasure of using a number of very engaging Belgian actors."

WHAT THE CRITICS SAID:

"Hypnotic. Absorbing. Provocative. Charged with erotic tension. Robinson Stévenin is riveting in the role. He is well-matched by Metzger's Johnny, whose brooding good looks and attitude are completely captivating. It makes this extraordinary film even more exceptional."

Toronto Gay & Lesbian Film Festival

"A psychosexual masterpiece that gets under your skin--and stays there."

Miami Gay & Lesbian Film Festival

CAST OF CHARACTERS

Robinson Stévenin (Bo Ancellin); Richard Bohringer (Detective Huysmans); Stéphane Metzger (Johnny); William Nadylam (Maeva); Frédéric Pellegeay (Alex); Ginette Garcin (Louisette Vincent); Stéphane de Groot (Pryzuski); Charles Dupont (Courtois); Veronica Novak (Elvire); Thibaut Corrion (Marléne); Marcel Dossogne (Professeur Ancellin); Micheline Presle (Violette Ancellin)

The Twenty Fourth (24th) Day

Written and Directed by Tony Piccirillo.
Produced by Nick Stagliano, Brad Medelsohn,
and Lou DiGiaimo Jr.
Released by Screen Media Ventures
in association with Nazz Productions.
Genre: Thriller
Runtime: 92 Minutes

PLOT SYNOPSIS:
Tom (Speedman) and Dan's (Marsden) one-night stand turns into an intensive power-play between captor and captive.

This film is a thriller. Actor Scott Speedman is cast as Tom, who as a married man has lived his whole life straight except for a one-night stand with a man five years ago. After getting diagnosed with HIV, he tracks down Dan, as played by James Marsden, the man he slept with. The question is this: was Dan responsible for infecting him?

Tom lures Dan back to his apartment where he ties him up and draws blood for an HIV test. If Dan tests positive, Tom claims he'll kill him. Thus, the stage is set for this battle of brain and brawn between two men locked in a studio apartment, perhaps both ultimately facing their deaths.

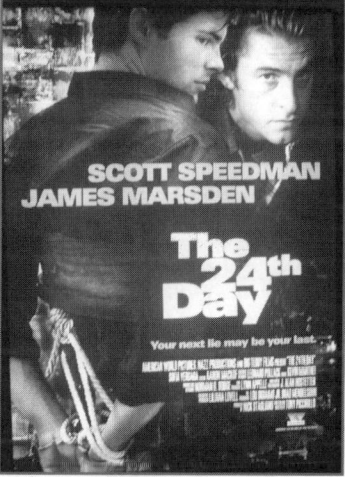
James Marsden and Scott Speedman

First launched as a play in Los Angeles, the script was considerably revamped for the screen. When *The 24th Hour* reached the screen, reviews were mixed: Some critics said it was a homophobic piece; others argue that it was just the opposite. That you must decide for yourself.

Even though this independent film, written and directed by Tony Piccirillo, has undergone many changes since it was inaugurated on the stage, there is still the lingering aura of a play about it. It follows the dark, conspiratorial genre of more successful, mainstream films, especially *Deathtrap* and *Sleuth*.

Tom has reason to be seriously agitated. He thinks that he infected his wife with the virus, a factor that contributed to her suicide after her discovery that she was ill.

If Dan is the guilty one, Tom reasons, "he must pay." Most of the drama centers around Dan's struggle to get the upper hand and to escape. The two men become engaged in a life-or-death psychological tug-of-war, and this holds much suspense for the viewer.

At some point, the conclusion becomes predictable, but interest in what's going to happen between the two men rarely lags. The faint-of-heart are warned about the strong language and what is called *adult situations* between two men. Perhaps the best things about *The 24th Day* are the two leading men, Scott Speedman from *Underworld* and James Marsden from *X-men*. Both actors handle their roles with skill and panache.

Despite scathing reviews from some critics, this is a well-acted, well-scripted, and riveting film. Few films have never dealt so effectively with the fear of HIV.

Scott Speedman

James Marsden

WHAT THE CRITICS SAID:

"Smugly poised Dan (James Marsden) goes home with rumpled, mumbly Tom (Scott Speedman), and the flirtatious banter gets awkward quickly. It transpires that the two had a one-night stand a few years back; Dan, apparently a slut, forgot. In the ensuing fog of embarrassment, Tom suddenly overpowers Dan, ties him up, and forcibly extracts a blood sample. Tom claims he's HIV-positive (he found that out 24 days ago, hence the title) and Dan is the only man he's ever slept with. Dan maintains he's been tested many times and is negative. And so begins a Death and the Maiden tango of culpability and vengeance in which the mantle of victimhood is lobbed back and forth like a ticking grenade."

Dennis Lim *Village Voice*

"Taking Dan back to his apartment, Tom suddenly turns shy, then sinister. This gay business, he says, is new to him. He's only slept with a man once before--five years ago--and that man he suspects was Dan. Insert first act curtain here. When we come back, Dan is Tom's prisoner, tied to a chair and forced to listen as Tom pours out his emotional history. It has been 24 days since Tom discovered that he had the AIDS virus. He believes that he passed the virus on to his wife, who committed suicide when she learned she was ill. Dan, says Tom, must pay. He draws a blood sample from his prisoner and submits it to a laboratory; if it comes back positive for H.I.V., Dan will die. Much of "The 24th Day" is devoted to a psychological tug-of-war, as Dan tries to get the upper hand by faking sympathy for Tom and drawing him into a personal conversation. (There is a long debate over who was the best Charlie's Angel--Kate Jackson or Farrah Fawcett--although the young protagonists would have barely been out of diapers at the time the show was on.)"

Dave Kehr *The New York Times*

"As you might imagine, a lot of impassioned arguments ensue, as Dan, in between escape attempts, employs a variety of psychological approaches to reasoning with his captor. In the course of their evening-length wrangle, Tom, who is married, reveals the personal tragedy that has led him to committing this act of violence.

The actors invest their performances with the requisite intensity, but for the most part fail to surprise us with their choices. Sofia Vergara also makes a brief appearance as Dan's roommate, in a role that seems obviously tacked on for this film version of the play, which was previously presented in a Los Angeles production starring Noah Wyle and Peter Berg."

Frank Scheck *The Hollywood Reporter*

PRODUCTION CREW:

Director of Photography: J. Alan Hostetter
Executive Producer: Liliana Lovell
Music: Kevin Manthei
Editors: Robert Larkin
                           Aaron Mackof
Production Designer: Norman Dodge
Costume Designer: Leonard Pollack

CAST OF CHARACTERS

James Marsden (Dan); Scott Speedman (Tom); Sofía Vergara (Isabella); Barry
Papick (Mr. Lerner); Charlie Corrado (Officer 1); Jarvis W. George (Officer 2);
Scott Roman (Bartender); Jeffrey Frost (Dan's Assistant); Jona Harvey (Marla);
Thea Chaloner (Wife); Brian Campbell (Blondie)

Twist

Written and Directed by Jacob Tierney.
Story by Charles Dickens.
Released by Strand Releasing
in association with Victorious Films,
Telefilm Canada, The Movie Network,
and Movie Central.
www.christalfilms.com/officialsites/twist
Genre: Drama
Runtime: 97 Minutes

PLOT SYNOPSIS:
*Twist is a calmly lucid retelling of Charles Dickens' classic **Oliver Twist**, updated to current times and moved out of the poor house and onto the street. Told from the point of view of the Artful Dodger (Dodge), Twist is no longer a tale of the misfortunes of boys, but rather about the prosaically beautiful Oliver who falls into the hands of down-and-out young men. Dodge takes the young man under his wing and instructs him in the unforgiving arts of drug abuse and prostitution. As Oliver's innocence dissolves, both young men confront inner demons and outer demons and, strangely, it is Dodge who finds he can't escape his past.*

The street is bitterly cold and dark. A cloud of warm breath comes from a shivering youth as he walks home after a night's work. This is *Twist*, the modern day retelling of Charles' Dickens' classic novel *Oliver Twist*.

Gone are the pickpockets and in their place are young men selling the most marketable commodity they have to offer--themselves. Gone too are the orphans and helpless victims of the 1800s and in their place the orphans of the dysfunctional families of the 1990s.

Told from the point of view of the Artful Dodger (Dodge), the setting of this famous novel is transported from England during the Industrial Revolution to present day, antiseptic Toronto, where life has all the appearance of being good.

Nick Stahl

Dodge, once at home in the suburbs of Montréal, is now a misanthropic veteran on the indifferent streets of Toronto. One evening, he meets Oliver who has run away from a lifetime of foster care. Dodge escorts him into the world of male prostitution, taking the young man under his wing, offering the tainted comforts of Fagin's den in return for implied compliance.

Touching, funny, poignant, and painful, Dodge and the other rent-boys are a family, less traditional, but more honest than the shattered illusions of Oliver's last home. Even Nancy, girlfriend of overlord Bill Sykes and dispenser of the drugs that keep the boys motivated, reaches out to Oliver with more warmth than he is accustomed.

As Oliver's innocence corrodes, Dodge becomes more and more distracted when he is stalked by his own brother David, a demon from his past. Oliver, too, seems to connect with his past in the form of a meeting with the Senator, a regular, who might just save him from his now inevitable fate. Meanwhile, Nancy's conscience breaks free from her paralyzing fear of Bill, and she decides she must finally reach out to her charges. Compelled to act on their instincts or wander in the urban wilderness forever, each of them confront their choices.

Faithful to the social tragedy that lay at the core of Dickens' writing--made more mournful in these enlightened times--*Twist* is about the creation of evil and the cyclical nature of violence that can keep even the bravest of us tangled in its web.

Joshua Close   Nick Stahl

Oliver Twist as a Male Hustler in Toronto

From its beginning, Charles Dickens' *Oliver Twist* has been a story of family--a created family, one which has fallen together as a refuge against a cruel world of reality. And in creating this sanctuary, it becomes a cruel reality in itself.

Actor-turned screenwriter/director, Jacob Tierney was admittedly one of the many for whom Charles Dickens' early classic, *Oliver Twist* was part of a common cultural memory. It is, after all, a classic for that very reason. But Jacob Tierney, 23 years old, raised in a family of filmmakers, is an individual who enjoys turning ideas inside out to see if truths are revealed. He found the temptation of retelling *Oliver Twist* with a modern twist irresistible.

Twist is removed from the innocence of Oliver's point of view and handed over to the Artful Dodger (Dodge, in this version) because Tierney feels this is a forgotten character in the book, one which conveys the underlying *gravitas* which has always been the story. "I went back to the text of the novel and looked at what wasn't discussed. Telling it with Dodge as the protagonist meant I had to give him a history," Tierney explains. "By making him the focus, it changed not only his arc, but the arc of the story too. Dickens was telling a tale of this one little perfect angel boy and I was telling the story of a dirty street boy who meets that perfect angel."

Take away the musical *bonhomie* that audiences associate with the 1968 family version and underneath lies a tragedy. But update it to present times and age the boys to the same as the teens you see living on the streets of every big city and it becomes a tragedy of transgressions usually left unmentioned. "This story is about the human condition, which is so taboo," says producer Victoria Hirst, who worked in tandem with Tierney from the early beginnings of this project. "And it's invigorating working with taboos because they require special handling. You don't want to run away from them, but storming up and confronting them head on doesn't work either. There is a responsibility to this kind of filmmaking because there is a fine line between making the point and making the point gratuitous."

When they first met, Hirst and Tierney connected immediately. They completely understood what the other person wanted and hoped for with this script. Hirst responded to Tierney's vision because of his "honesty, integrity, creativity, and clarity of intent. It was his attachment to the material and sheer drive to tell his story that I found inspirational."

Oliver Twist as a Male Hustler
in Toronto (cont'd)

Tierney offers a tour through the storyline, "We open on Dodge, a hustler and a junkie. Nancy works at the Three Cripples' Diner and facilitates the drug trade for her boyfriend, Bill (Sykes) who provides a group of rent-boys with heroin while they work the streets. Part of Dodge's job is to recruit new boys. He discovers Oliver killing time alone in a coffee shop and with the manipulative invitation of somewhere to spend the night, Dodge takes him back to Fagin's loft. Slowly Oliver is inducted into the lifestyle of male hustlers. One night he meets the Senator, one of the regular johns, played by Stephen McHattie. The Senator is a 'talker' and in the course of an evening, he suspects Oliver is the son of his daughter who ran away from home at 15. Meanwhile, a car from Québec stalks Dodge, but he refuses to share his problems with anyone. We discover that the stalker is Dodge's brother, David, who has tracked him down after he ran away from his well-to-do family a year earlier. Their father had abused both the boys, and David now needs to find Dodge in order to deal with his own issues and seek forgiveness."

Tierney continues with his description of the story, "Nancy gets involved in trying to save Oliver and redeem her own life. She's a character who has figured out that to survive with a man like Bill, passivity and compliance will keep her alive physically, even if it has already killed her emotionally. Do nothing--avoid everything. When she meets Oliver, she is touched by his purity of heart and recklessly seizes this opportunity to act. What she chooses to do is encourage Oliver to connect with a client, the Senator (whom we are led to believe could be his grandfather), and accept his offer of escape. Nancy does not necessarily believe it will end happily, but it's as if in trying to save Oliver from this life, she is also trying to prevent the death of hope. That's makes Oliver special--he believes people are good and Nancy thinks that if Oliver doesn't call the Senator, it's because the hope in him has died."

PRODUCTION CREW:

Director of Photography:	Gerald Packer
Executive Producers:	Dan Lyon and Kevin Tierney
Music:	Ron Proulx
Editor:	Mitch Lackie
Production Designer:	Ethan Tobman
Costume Designer:	Joanna Syrokomla

WHAT THE CRITICS SAID:

"Mr. Tierney's update imagines Oliver as a blond virginal teenager (Joshua Close) who has run away from a grim life in the provinces to the big city. On his first night in town he is lucky enough to run into Dodge (Nick Stahl), a youthful prostitute who takes him back to the dormitory for lost boys operated by Fagin (Gary Farmer)."

Dave Kehr *The New York Times*

"Although his is unlike any other version of the story ever filmed and despite a tendency to wallow in the sordidness of it all, Tierney (best known for his role in *The Neon Bible*), clearly has talent, not least is getting fine performances from his actors. Oliver, played by newcomer Joshua Close, is a rent-boy in this version of the story but the emphasis is as much on the character of the Artful Dodger, called simply Dodge, and played with riveting intensity by Nick Stahl, as it is on Close's handsome, soulful Oliver."

David Stratton *Variety*

"*Twist* is the second movie in recent years to mess around with Dickens by transporting his novels to modern times. As an update of *Oliver Twist*, it is more inspired than the contemporary take on *Great Expectations*, which was far from great and failed to live up to the expectations created by a high-tone director, Alfonso Cuaron, and a cast headed by Gwyneth Paltrow and Robert DeNiro."

Carla Meyer and Ruthe Stein *San Francisco Chronicle*

"Nick Stahl, a talented young actor who seems to specialize in playing angst-ridden youth, stars as Dodge, a young male-prostitute and junkie whose boss, the violent Fagin, keeps a stable of such young looking boys. When Dodge came across the innocent looking Oliver, a runaway from suburbia, he enlists him into the fold, with predictably melodramatic results."

Franck Scheck *The Hollywood Reporter*

CAST OF CHARACTERS

Nick Stahl (Dodge); Joshua Close (Oliver); Gary Farmer (Fagin); Michelle-Barbara Pelletier (Nancy); Tygh Runyan (David); Stephen McHattie (The Senator); Moti Yona (Charley); Brigid Tierney (Betsy); Max McCabe (Noah); Andre Noble (Adam); James Gilpin (Aide); Josh Holliday (Morris); Mike Lobel (Bully); Michael Ripley (John); Caroline Sura (Girl); Emily Hampshire (Waitress)

The Original Oliver Twist

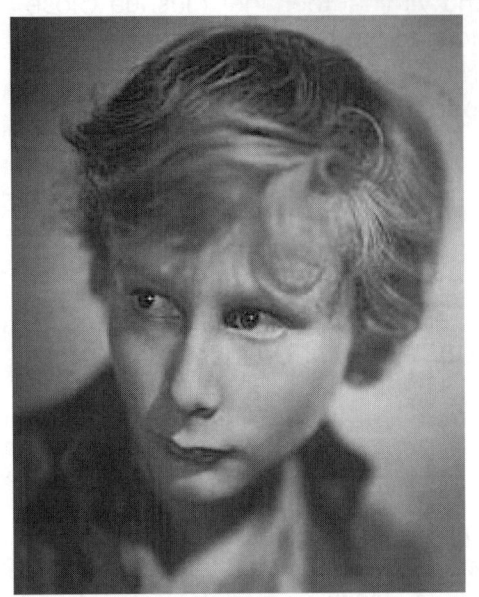

John Howard Davies (1948)

Joshua Close

Wasabi Tuna

Directed by Lee Freidlander.
Written by Celia Fox.
Produced by Celia Fox, Lee Friedlander,
and Clayton Keiber.
Released by Genesis Films
in association with Creative Alley Productions.
www.wasabituna.com and
www.creativealleyproductions.com
Genre: Action, Comedy
Runtime: 93 Minutes

PLOT SYNOPSIS:
A group of friends who take Halloween too seriously kidnap Anna Nicole Smith's beloved pet Sugar-Pie. It's up to a bunch of drag queens, each dressed as Anna, to bring Sugar-Pie back.

This urban caper—packed with action—takes place in Los Angeles the night before Halloween. Naturally, everyone, especially drag queens, is rushing to put the finishing touches on their costumes.

The cast faces a dilemma of what to wear for the big, brash block party, otherwise known as the West Hollywood Halloween Parade. Fredrico is Antonio Sabato Jr. cast as a hot young Latino spinning instructor. Dave, as played by Tim Meadows, is a rising African-American stockbroker. The stylish young interior designer, Evan, is portrayed by Jason London. Harvey is Evan's fabulous business partner and main squeeze, as played by Barney Cheng.

Other members of the cast include Emme (Alanna Ubach), a quirky young woman obsessed with old movies and fashion. Puzzled as to what to be for Halloween, this murky crew decides to appear

Alexis Arquette, Yuda Acco, Raymond Jones, and Clint Childs

dressed up as gangbangers, like those seen on the kill-or-be-killed streets of East Los Angeles. In other words, they want to look "straight from the 'hood." To achieve some semblance of truth, they decide to learn from the professionals themselves.

One of those professionals is a character named Romeo (Guillermo Diaz), a real life gangster in the film. He agrees to lend Dave his purple lowrider in exchange for Dave's cherry-red Porsche.

What follows is a series of mishaps involving vengeful gangbangers, police chases, surveillance teams, drug lords, even a team of Anna Nicole Smith drag queens. It's a farce and hilarious. Of course, the star of the show is Sugar-Pie, Anna Nicole's pet dog.

Expect flying fists and wigs in the bar brawls that follow—all in good, gay fun. But time behind bars looms in the future. View *Wasabi Tuna* as a romp and a caper comedy. This will certainly lead off the genre of future drag queen kidnapping action-comedies.

In many ways, *Wasabi Tuna*, evokes a John Waters film, especially *Pink Flamingos* where Divine ate dog shit. Any remake of *Flamingos* should star Anna Nicole herself. She does, in fact, appear in *Wasabi Tuna* as herself (who else?).

Wasabi Tuna: Post Rocky, Post Priscilla
An interview with Writer Celia Fox
(Interview by Fred Topel)

Question: How did you conceive of the tone?
Celia Fox: I wanted to do something real light and fun, that definitely had a *Rocky Horror Show* or *Priscilla, Queen of the Desert* kind of feel to it, that was real bright colors and that was light. I saw a lot of heavy movies and a lot of dreary movies coming out, and I was a little burned out myself.

Q: Is comedy a risk in indies, because you limit your audience if they don't share the sense of humor?
CF: I definitely think it is a risk. It's not a Sundance film. You limit yourself in the film festivals automatically. It's a huge risk. It's much easier to get a type of audience doing a movie, say, *Thirteen* or *Monster's Ball* because you definitely target an audience, you know the film festivals are going to accept that. But comedy also is, on the flip side, worldwide. And it's what I wanted to do with my background. It's what I felt comfortable in, the media I felt comfortable with, so it was natural to me.

Antonio Sabato Jr.

Anna Nicole Smith

Alanna Ubach

PRODUCTION CREW:

Director of Photography:	Ben Kufrin
Executive Producer:	Celia Fox
Editors:	Larry Madaras and Ken Morrisey
Production Designer:	Yuda Acco
Costume Designer:	Shon LeBlanc

CAST OF CHARACTERS

Lisa Arning (Chic Sales Girl); Christian Kieber (Becker); Frederico Dordei (Sark); Johnny Williams (Wally); Dariush Kashani (Mahdi); Alexis Arquette(Santa Ana Anna); Jason Boggs (Butchie); Megan Cavanagh (Megan); Barney Chang (Harvey); Troy DeWalt (Gay Cowboy); Guillermo Diaz (Romeo); Arturo Gil (Eenie Santa Ana); Leslie Jordan (Sam); Crystal Kwon (Monique); Jason London (Evan); Irina Maleeva (Mrs. Hasadan); Tim Meadows (Dave); Antonio Sabato Jr. (Fredrico); Anna Nicole Smith (as Herself); Alanna Ubach (Emme)

Yes Nurse! No Nurse!

(Ja zuster, nee zuster)

Written by Harry Bannink
and Frank Houtappels.
Directed by Pieter Kramer.
Produced by Burny Bos,
Peter Jan Brouwer, Michiel de Rooij,
and Sabine Veenendaal.
Released by Bos Bro. Film/TV Productions
in association with Here! Films
www.yesnursenonurse.com
Genre: Comedy/Musical
Runtime: 100 Minutes
Dutch with English subtitles

PLOT SYNOPSIS:
Cheerful and campy, this is a stylized musical comedy, sung and acted in Dutch, that evokes and mimics, the golden age of Hollywood musicals. The plot unfolds within the boarding house of Sister Klivia. The kind-hearted occupants of Sister Klivia's rest home is contrasted by the nasty and frequently complaining next-door neighbor, Herr Boordeval, who has searched for years for a reason to shut down the guesthouse. One day, a female occupant of the guesthouse meets a handsome young guy named Gerrit. Sister Klivia lets him stay despite the fact that he is a thief. Will Gerrit's presence within the guesthouse lend weight to the accusations of Herr Boordeval?

This musical parody is a bit of camp – in fact, "Beyond the Valley of Camp." It's a parody of those Debbie Reynolds movies that MGM turned out in the 1950s. Naturally, it's colored like cheap candy and very sitcommy.

A light, breezy tone is maintained throughout. The script was also based on a popular TV series in the Netherlands back in the 1960s. Many critics lampooned the idea of trying to "be a euphonious entertainment in one of the world's most uneuphonious languages." This may be the only Dutch musical ever made but, in spite of that, the talented cast carries on valiantly. Expect no fewer than ten musical numbers, which are greater than the weak plot.

Loes Luca

Such as it is, the plot spins around the rift between the quirky occupants of a rest home and its misanthropic landlord.

Can a Dutch musical cross international borders? That is the question. One movie-goer claimed that he went along with a friend who wanted to see the movie. He had no desire to watch it but was caught up in its spell claiming that it was a "great movie with great acting."

Other viewers of the film have not always been that enthusiastic. *The New York Times* was particularly cruel, claiming that, "The waltz-heavy score by Raymond Van Santen and Ferdinand Boland sounds like *Mamma Mia* for preschoolers, with bubble-headed ditties that include a tribute to granddads, a joining-the-circus fantasy, a Greek dancing pastiche, and an ode to one character's 17 pet pigeons."

The ghost of Busby Berkeley hangs over the choreography. That is not necessarily a bad thing.

If you like a madcap tale set in the world's zaniest rest home, you've probably made the right choice of a flick.

Paul de Leeuw

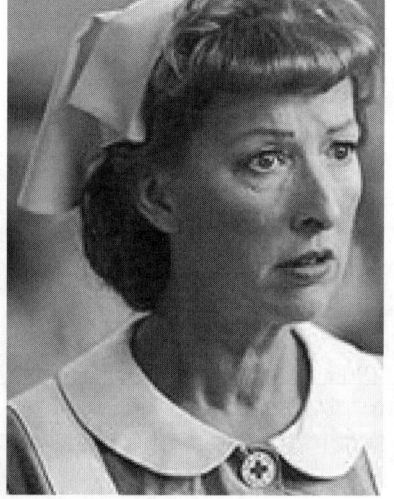
Loes Luca

Paul Kooij

PRODUCTION CREW:

Director of Photography: Poitr Kukla
Music: Raymund Van Santen
Editor: Elja De Lange
Production Designer: Vincent De Pater
Art Designer: Albert Kuipers
Production Management: Jean-Pierre Claes and Arjan Eekels
Assistant Directors: Jonas Hendrix, Maud Kieft, Willem Quarles and Van Ufford

WHAT THE CRITICS SAID:

"Following the bright main title, with whit-garbed nurses in a Busby Berkeley homage, the movie's opening is promising, as pretty young thing Jet (Tjitske Reidinga) is courted on her way home in the rain by handsome Gerrit (Waldemar Torenstra). Sequence plays as a cross between "The Umbrellas of Cherbourg" and "Singin' in the Rain" in inspiration and poster-color look, and there's a lightness to the number and a cheerful cheesiness to the lyric ("Together with a fella/Under one umbrella") that's just right."

Derek Elley *Variety*

"One of the most appealing aspects of the film is its set, made to look like a busy street brimming with flashy early-'60s colors and fashions. The choreographed numbers performed here clop along with English-sounding consonants and are really silly as they are catchy. (All together now: "Twip, twip, twip/don't crash into the piano or you'll slip.")"

John McMurtrie *San Francisco Chronicle*

"The madcap residents, none of whom seem to get any rest, include a wild-eyed inventor who fantasizes about winning a Nobel Prize after his peppermint flavored happy pill turns a savage house cat into an inert lump of purring sweetness. When Boordevol is slipped the pill in the courtroom where he is pursuing a case against the rest home, the teeth-gnashing grinch briefly turns into a giddy apostle of sweetness and light."

Stephen Holden *New York Times*

"A candy-colored update of a Dutch TV series from the 60s, *Yes Nurse! No Nurse!* Has an occasional from-Mars appeal, as the mildly cracked denizens of the rest home (say it with me: rusthuis) run by nurse Klivia (Loes Luca) burst into song with cheerful abandon. Styles range from cabaret to barbershop to toe-tapping bubblegum, and the rain-day serenade at the start nods Cherbourgward, with a soupcon of Low Countries sass ("But walk a little faster, please/I badly need the loo")."

Ed Park *Village Voice*

"The cast is energetic and broad in sitcom style, and director Pieter Kramer and co-writer Frank Houtappels, like their actors and have the courage of the saccharine, zany silliness of their material."

Kevin Thomas *Los Angeles Times*

WHAT THE CRITICS SAID (CONT'D):

"Cheerfully goofy if over long, *Yes Nurse! No Nurse!* is a campy, brightly colored musical comedy based on a popular '60s Dutch sitcom that's unlike any other film out there. Director Pieter Kramer offers up no few than 10 production numbers, the best of them at the beginning: a Busby Berkeley-style opening sequence, and an homage to "Singin' in the Rain" and "The Umbrellas of Cherbourg" featuring the movie's lovers, Tjitske Reidinga (as Klivia's daughter) and Waldemar Torenstra (as a kleptomaniac)."

Lou Lumenick *New York Post*

"Let's start by writing a disclaimer for *Ja zuster, nee zuster* (*Yes Nurse, No Nurse*): This wacky, campy lampoon of 1950s Hollywood musicals is not for everyone. Not for those who think that early John Waters – *Hairspray, Polyester* – is overrated. And definitely not for those who take the American musical films of the past as sacred art that shouldn't be tampered with. But inspired by Waters' over-the-top musical comedies and adding touches of easily recognized films (did I see a send-up of *Singin' in the Rain*?), *Yes Nurse, No Nurse* is fun – if you get into its groove."

Marta Barber *Miami Herald*

"*Yes Nurse, No Nurse* has some great *Singin' in the Rain* retro numbers, excellent storylines about miracle drugs that turn grumpy misers into lovable teddy bears, and a remarkable sense of silly style. The film isn't completely contemporary – there's an old-fashioned spirit to the overall flow of the picture that moves as if *Xanadu* and all unavoidably postmodern movie musicals that came after it never happened – but it ain't no homage, either."

Mike Restaino *Entertainment Today*

CAST OF CHARACTERS

Loes Luca (Sister Klivia); Paul Kooij (Neighbor Boordevol); Tjitske Reidinga (Jet); Waldemar Torenstra (Gerrit); Paul de Leeuw (Wouter); Beppe Costa (Engineer); Edo Brunner (Bertus); Lennart Vader (Bobby); Frits Lambrechts (Opa); Olga Zuiderhoek (Rechter); Arjan Ederveen (Choreographer); Pierre van Duijl (Greek); Guus Dam (Agent 1); Joep Onderdelinden (Agent 2); Ad Knippels (SRV Boss)

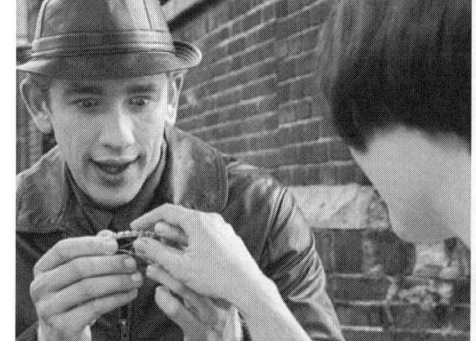

You I Love

Written by Olga Stolpovskaya.
Directed by Olga Stolpovskaya
and Dmitry Troitsky.
Produced by Dmitry Troitsky.
Released by Picture This! Entertainment.
www.picturethisent.com/minisites/youilove
Genre: Comedy
Runtime: 86 Minutes
Russian with English subtitles

PLOT SYNOPSIS:
Three young Muscovites – two men and a woman – appear in this story of post-millennium Russia. The beautiful TV newsreader, Vera, meets and falls in love with Tim, who's in advertising. Their love grows stronger day by day until, presto, Uloomji, a young almond-eyed Kalmyk, appears in their bed. Tim has also fallen for this exotic creature. The fun is about to begin.

This is a comedy love-story about the lives of the young Muscovites today.

Vera, a beautiful TV newsreader, meets and falls in love with Tim, an advertising man. Luckily, he falls in love with her also.

They have much in common: they are under-paid, overworked and severely stressed.

Evgeny Koryakovsky and Damir Badmaev

Tim and Vera's relationship seems to have some healing power for them as their love grows stronger, but on the day of their first anniversary dinner, Vera comes home to find Tim in bed with Uloomji – a young Kalmyk male. And then the events begin to spin well out of the control for our heroes. The whirlwind pace of modern-day Moscow never allows them a moment to pause, think, understand…

The style is slick, young and ultra-cool. The story urges forward with sudden twists and unpredictable turns of events.

This film demonstrated that for the new generation of Russians love is the same crazy feeling it was, except that now, they can be more open about it… or, can they?

The film is an attempt to satirize Russia's post-communist economic landscape. But, we are not sure that homophobia in modern day Russia can be treated in a way that's as jaunty as this film suggests. Gay backlash may not be as severe today in Russia as it is in Red State America, but, even so, it is hardly a laughing matter.

The performances are adequate but without screams for the Academy Awards to recount their choices. There are evocative touches, including that of a Kalmyk day worker who cleans cages at the Moscow Zoo, while secretly harboring a dream of being a circus acrobat.

This unorthodox film may be a harbinger of what is to come for Russian filmmakers who will inhabit a landscape far different from what most of them were born into.

Damir Badmaev

Evgeny Koryakovsky

Lubov Tolkalina

PRODUCTION CREW:

Director of Photography: Aleksandr Simonov
Production Designer: Konstantin Vitavsky
Costume Designer: Anastasia Nefedova
Music: Richardas Norvila
Editors: Sergey Pluschenko and Oleg Raevsky
Sound: Alexandr Abramov
Production Manager: Larisa Shlepina

WHAT THE CRITICS SAID:

"Viewers who know Russia through movies by Sergei Eisenstein and Andrei Terkovsky would not recognize the Moscow depicted in *You I Love*. According to the off-beat sex comedy, Moscow is filled with chic, elegant people with money to spend on the finer things of life. Director-writer Olga Stolpovskaya uses jump cuts, flashy graphics and cool techno music to paint a delightful portrait of a post-Communist Russia overdosing on capitalism. *You I Love* is like an early Almodóvar movie transported to Moscow."

V.A. Musetto New York Post

"*You I Love* is not without its loopy charms. Indeed, the film is most buoyant when most over-the-top – there's a fetishistic scene in which Vera gets a body treatment that appears to be a cross between bondage and electroconvulsive shock therapy. Given the attractive leads and the casual, utopian take on queer sexuality – anathema to the "moral values" crowd – there are worse ways to while away these gloomy post-election days."

Joshua Land Village Voice

"The opening sequence of Olga Stolpovskaya and Dmitry Troitsky's glossy *You I Love* suggest that the filmmakers are intent on creating the impression that their romantic comedy could just as easily be unfolding in New York as in Moscow. The settings are sleek, modern and upscale, accented with glimpses of towering vintage landmark buildings. Its stars, Lubov Tolkalina and Evgeny Koryakovsky, are young and attractive."

Kevin Thomas Los Angeles Times

"After he meets a young illegal worker, everything changes for Moscow metrosexual and ad exec Timofei (Evgeny Koryakovsky), who's involved with gorgeous news anchor Vera (Lubov Tolkalina). Actually, Uloomji (Damir Badmaev), a zoo worker with circus aspirations, crashes into Timofei's car while practicing his trapeze routine on a city street. With no real place of his own, Uloomji recuperates from his fall in Timofei's glam apartment – and, with an innocent acrobatic zeal, puts the moves on his host in one of the wackiest seduction scenes in recent memory."

Sheri Linden Hollywood Reporter

CAST OF CHARACTERS

Damir Badmaev (Uloomji); Lubov Tolkalina (Vera Kirillova); Evgeny Koryakovsky (Timofei Pechorin); Irina Grineva (Make-up girl); Emanuel Michael Vaganda (Jone); Yury Sherstnev (Watchman at the zoo); Victor Shevidov (Uncle Vanya); Nina Agapova (Neighbor old lady); Michail Tarabukin (Lyolik)

You'll Get Over It
(Tu Verras Ça Te Passera)

Written by Vincent Molina.
Directed by Fabrice Cazeneuve.
Produced by Hervé Chabalier,
Claude Chelli and Christophe Chevallier.
Released by Capa Drama in association with
Picture This! Entertainment.
www.picturethisent.com
Genre: Drama
Runtime: 90 Minutes
French with English subtitles

PLOT SYNOPSIS:
When Vincent finds himself a victim of outing in his high school, he must accept to live with the drastic changes it provokes, and redefine his relationships with his friends and family.

In the French coming-of-age drama *You'll Get Over It* (*Tu Verras Ça Te Passera*), popular 16-year-old high school student Vincent (Julien Baumgartner) stars on the swim team and dates a pretty girl named Noémie (Julia Maraval). His family, his teachers, his coach all love and admire him, but in one respect, he's misleading them all. This becomes all too apparent when Benjamin (*Come Undone's* Jérémie Elkaïm) moves to town, and, seeing through Vincent's façade, pursues him.

Julien Baumgartner and Jérémie Elkaïm

Vincent's classmates see the two of them together, rumors abound, and somebody completes the "outing" process by spray painting "Vincent is a fag" on one of the schoolyard walls. The swim team ostracizes Vincent, his closest friends are angry about the deceptions, and his parents don't know what to say. Perhaps it's too much for a 16-year-old kid to sort out himself.

Jérémie Elkaïm starred previously in the very successful gay romance *Come Undone* as a troubled young man coping with his sexuality. In *You'll Get Over It*, he takes a role on the other side of the coming-out equation, that of openly gay Benjamin. Elkaïm's previous films include Stephane Kanzadjian's *Sexy Boys*, a French take on *American Pie*, and Catherine Corsini's The *Very Merry Widows* starring Jane Birkin.

Another star of *Sexy Boys*, Julien Baumgartner, teams up again with Jérémie Elkaïm for *You'll Get Over It*. Appearing regularly on French television, his work includes *Un Beau Jour*, *Un Coiffeur* and *La Tranchée des Espoirs*.
You'll Get Over It is directed by acclaimed TV and film director Fabrice Cazeneuve. His

recent works include the films *Un Fils De Notre Temps* and *La Dette*. He also won the Sliver Leopard Award at the Locarno International Film Festival for his film *The King of China*.

The actors portray their characters with sensitivity and depth, turning in nuanced performances. Of course, this coming-of-age theme has been worked a lot in both film and books, but it appears new again in this retelling. The script is presumably autobiographical.

Jérémie Elkaïm

Julien Baumgartner and Jérémie Elkaïm

PRODUCTION CREW:

Director of Photography: Stephan Massis
Music: Michel Potal
Editor: Jean-Pierre Bloc
Production Designer: Olivier Raoux
Costume Designers: Marie-José Escolar and Isabelle Vita
Assistant Directors: Jeanna Crespin and George Every
Sound: Bruno Charier, Laurent Dreyer, Patrick Egreteau, Mathieu Weber, and Béatrice Wick

WHAT THE CRITICS SAID:

"This fast-paced, well-acted film brings emotional integrity to a familiar tale."

Chuck Wilson *LA Weekly*

"*You'll Get Over It* is a universal and wholly original tale of our times that will speak to anyone who has ever struggled with hopes, insecurities, and disappointments on the way to self-determination."

Sensory Perceptions, Portland Gay & Lesbian Film Festival

"Director Cazeneuve reveals himself to be a master of the simplified moment, bringing the headier sociological issues of the story into a theatrical, emotional context that is both accessible and absorbing. Resonates with earnest truthfulness and packs a surprising dramatic punch!"

Gabriel Shanks *Mixed Reviews*

"The film couldn't be more honest or compassionate in depicting the handsome sensitive teenager's coming out story."

Dennis Schwartz *Ozus' World*

"A sensitive and realistic look on the "dangerous passage" called youth."

Le Monde

"Strong and insightful, *You'll Get Over It* approaches with realism and intelligence the delicate subject of homosexuality."

France Soir

"Julien Baumgartner is a compelling screen presence!"

Leah Greenblatt, *TimeOut NY*

"A surprisingly frank and candid story of one teenager's coming out."

SF International Lesbian & Gay Film Fest

CAST OF CHARACTERS

Julien Baumgartner (Vincent); Julia Maraval (Noémie); François Comar (Stéphane); Jérémie Elkaïm (Benjamin); Patrick Bonnel (Bernard, the Father); Christiane Millet (Sylvie); Antoine Michel (Régis, the Brother); Nils Ohlund (Bruno); Bernard Blancan (Swimming Coach); Eric Bonicatto (French Professor)

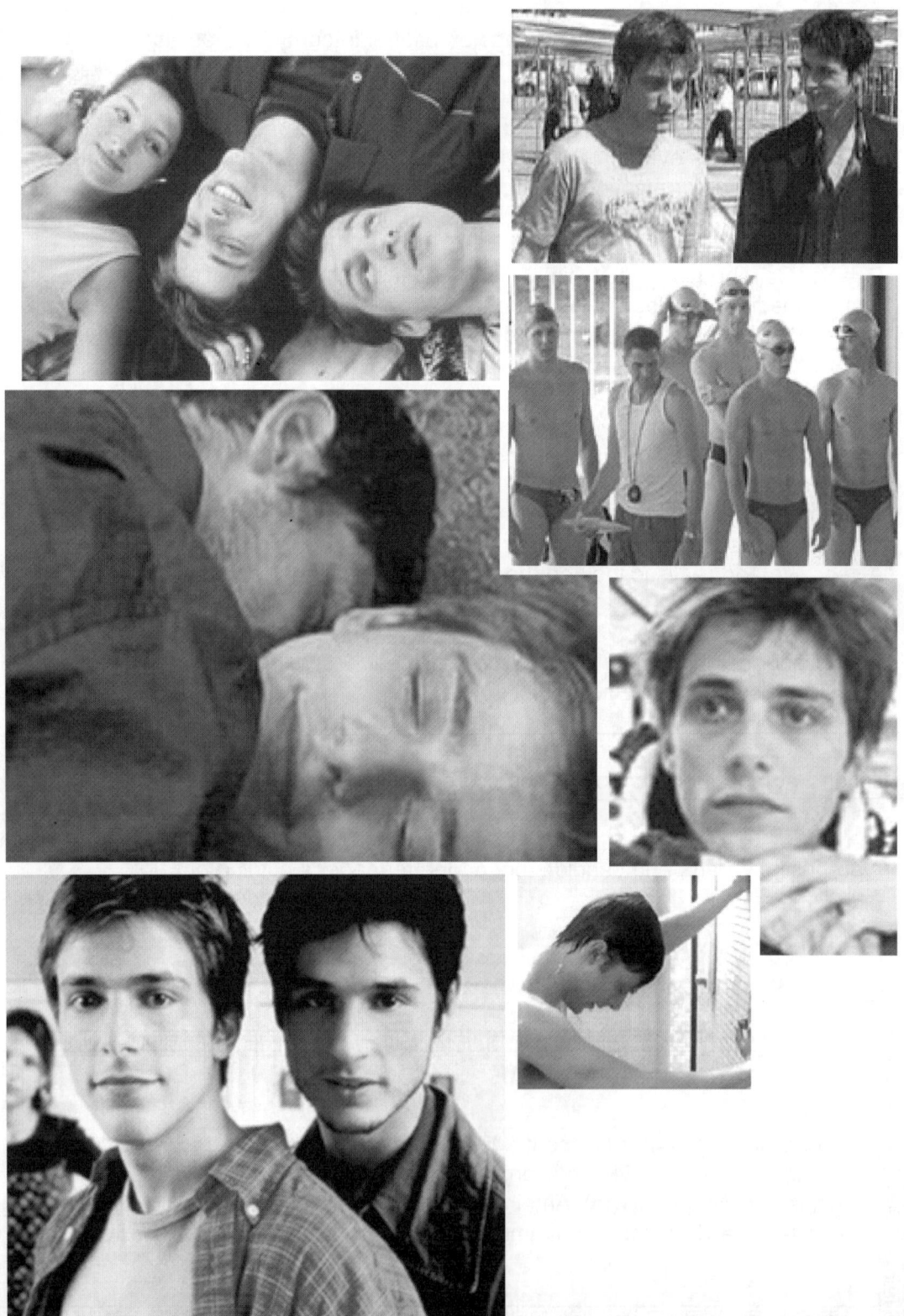

 **Coming soon: A film worth waiting for.**

Entertainment Now! Hot, provocative, and pithy

BLOOD MOON PRODUCTIONS

Specializing in the transcription of oral histories
that change America's ways of interpreting
its cinematic past.

What is
Blood Moon Productions?

Founded in 1997 as
The Georgia Literary Association, and now
based in New York City,
it's a small-scale publishing venture that's
staffed with writers and editors
who otherwise devote their energies to
THE FROMMER GUIDES, one of the
best-known names in travel publishing.

Blood Moon, however,
also extends deep into the history of
the entertainment industry.

In April of 2005, the official newsletter of
**New York's Small Press Center for
Independent Publishing** described us like this:

"Established by a consortium of professional
journalists, Blood Moon Productions has
carved its niche by publishing provocative
biographies of the stars who reigned during
Hollywood's Golden Age"

For an idea of some of our previous endeavors
(those not related to travel), please refer to the
following pages, or visit us on the web.

www.BloodMoonProductions.com

The Secret Life of
Humphrey Bogart
The Early Years
(1899 - 1931)
Darwin Porter

Loaded with information once suppressed by the Hollywood studios, this is the most revealing book ever written about the undercover lives of the Movie Stars of the 1930s. Learn what America's most visible male star was doing during his mysterious early years on Broadway and in Hollywood at the dawn of the Talkies--details that Bogie worked hard to suppress during his later years with Bacall.

The subject of more than 80 radio interviews by its author, and widely covered by both the tabloids and the mainstream press, it's based on never-before-published memoirs, letters, diaries, and interviews from men and women who either loved him or who wanted him to burn in hell. No wonder Bogie, in later life, never wanted to talk about his early years.

Serialized in three parts by Britain's *Mail on Sunday*, with some of its revelations flashed as news events around the world, it demonstrates that Hollywood's Golden Age stars were human, highly sexed, and at least when they were with other Hollywood insiders, remarkably indiscreet.

WHAT THE CRITICS SAID:

This biography has had us pondering as to how to handle its revelations within a town so protective of its own...This biography of Bogart's early years is exceptionally well-written.   JOHN AUSTIN, *HOLLYWOOD INSIDE*

In this new biography, we learn about how Bogart struggled for stardom in the "anything goes" era of the Roaring 20s.   *THE GLOBE*

Porter's book uncovers scandals within the entertainment industry of the 1920s and 1930s, when publicists from the movie studios deliberately twisted and suppressed inconvenient details about the lives of their emerging stars."   *TURNER CLASSIC MOVIE NEWS*

This biography brilliantly portrays a slice of time: In this case, the scandal-soaked days of Prohibition, when a frequently hung-over Bogie operated somwhat like a blank sheet of paper on which other actors, many of them infamous, were able to design their lives. The book is beautifully written.   LAURENCE HAZELL, PhD. University of Durham (UK)

KATHARINE THE GREAT:

A LIFETIME OF SECRETS REVEALED....   BY DARWIN PORTER

A highly controversial trade paperback from **Blood Moon Productions**.
558 pages, with an index and at least 70 vintage photos.
ISBN 0-9748118-0-7 $16.95   FIRST EDITION PUBLISHED IN 2004

KATHARINE HEPBURN WAS A BELOVED AND MUCH-RESPECTED
ICON OF THE AMERICAN THEATER.
YOU'VE READ WHAT **KATE REMEMBERED**: HERE'S WHAT SHE WANTED TO FORGET.

Katharine
The Great

a lifetime
of secrets...
revealed by Darwin Porter

WHAT THE CRITICS SAID:

"Behind the scenes of her movies, Katharine Hepburn played the temptress to as many women as she did men, ranted and raved with her co-stars and directors, and broke into her neighbors' homes for fun. <u>And somehow, she managed to keep all of it out of the press.</u> As they say, Katharine the Great is hard to put down."
DALLAS VOICE, April, 2004

"Page by page, chapter by chapter, this carefully researched and documented *Katharine the Great* sheds light on America's icon of feminist strength, with her chiseled beauty and patrician bearing. The lights of Broadway dimmed to honor Hepburn's death, but the bulbs are turned on again in this startling book. In explicit detail, the book documents not only the two great loves of Hepburn's life, Laura Harding and Spencer Tracy, but her minor affairs off-camera as well."
A DIFFERENT LIGHT (Los Angeles)

"Author Darwin Porter, following his remarkable 2003 book on the private life of Humphrey Bogart, has surpassed himself with this incredibly detailed biography of one of the 20th century's premier stage and movie stars. 'Write anything about me you like,' she told Porter, 'just don't ever tell the truth.' Sorry Kate---Here comes the truth."
THE TRI-STATE REVIEW

"The door to Hepburn's closet has finally been opened. This is the most honest and least apologetic biography of Hollywood's most ferociously private actress ever written."
BOOMER TIMES / SENIOR LIFE MAGAZINE (Boca Raton, Florida)

In Porter's biography of Katharine Hepburn, details about the inner workings of a movie studio (RKO in the early 30s), are relished. The book even offers insights into the phobias of Howard Hughes.--Oh boy, do I remember Mama!)
CONRAD DOERR in THE BOTTOM LINE (Palm Springs, California)

KATHARINE THE GREAT WAS NOMINATED BY <u>FOREWORD MAGAZINE</u>, A PROMINENT LITERARY
REVIEW, AS ONE OF TEN FINALISTS FOR **BEST BIOGRAPHY** OF 2004

RHINESTONE COUNTRY by Darwin Porter

A tender but provocative portrait of America's country-western music industry and some of the singers who clawed their way to stardom. Sweeping across the racial and sexual landscapes of the Deep South, it takes a hard look at closeted lives south of the Mason-Dixon line and the destructive aspects of fame.

Delectable and tantalizing!

"A sexual kick in the groin. High-adrenaline love, violence, and betrayal. Indulge yourself with this one. Darwin Porter has done it again with this riveting show-biz tale of fame and lust."
-Tyrone Maxwell

GEORGIA LITERARY ASSOCIATION

FROM THE GEORGIA LITERARY ASSOCIATION
ISBN 0-9668030-3-5 PAPERBACK $15.95

From the Georgia Literary Association, in cooperation with the Florida Literary Association, a reprint of the bestselling cult classic.

ISBN 1-877978-95-7. Paperback $12.95

BUTTERFLIES IN HEAT

THE LONG-AWAITED RETURN OF THE CULT CLASSIC-- ONE OF THE BEST-SELLING GLBT NOVELS OF ALL TIME.

A study in malevolence, vendetta, morbid fascination, and redemption. One of the very few pop novels ever praised by Tennessee Williams ("I'd walk the waterfront for Numie any day...."), it was the inspiration for the original character of the male prostitute as portrayed by Jon Voight in *Midnight Cowboy*. Its hero is blond god Numie Chase, an unlucky hustler with flesh to sell.

"Darwin Porter writes with an incredible understanding of the milieu--hot enough to singe the wings off any butterfly."

--James Kirkwood, co-author, *A Chorus Line*

"How does Darwin Porter's garden grow? Only in the moonlight, and only at midnight,when man-eating vegetation in any color but green bursts into full bloom to devour the latest offerings."

James Leo Herlihy, author of *MIDNIGHT COWBOY*

"Not since I saw Tennessee Williams's first Broadway play have I experienced such a compelling American writer."

--*Greta Keller*

BLOOD MOON

FROM THE GEORGIA LITERARY ASSOCIATION.
ISBN 0-9668030-4-3 $10.99

SET WITHIN THE GLITTERY AND SOMETIMES TAWDRY CONTEXT OF SOUTH FLORIDA, THIS IS THE ABRIDGED VERSION OF DARWIN PORTER'S MOST SUCCESSFUL EROTIC THRILLER. IT'S ABOUT LOVE, PSYCHOSIS, SEXUAL OBSESSION, PORNOGRAPHY, POWER, AND RELIGIOUS FANATICISM IN AMERICA TODAY. ITS TITLE (AND SALES RECORD) INSPIRED OUR CHOICE OF **BLOOD MOON PRODUCTIONS** AS THE NAME OF OUR PUBLISHING HOUSE AFTER ITS REORGANIZATION IN 2003. AND BECAUSE OF RECENT REVELATIONS ABOUT THE LINKS BETWEEN THE REGIME OF GEORGE W. BUSH AND THE SAUDI OIL EMPIRE, ITS PLOT AND MANY OF ITS THEN-SHOCKING PREMISES (ORIGINALLY PUBLISHED IN AN EXPANDED EDITION IN 1999) NOW SEEM ALMOST CLAIRVOYANT. AND ITS ENDING REVEALS WHAT REALLY HAPPENS WHEN THE MOON TURNS TO BLOOD.

"Rose Phillips, **Blood Moon**'s charismatic and deviant evangelist, and her uncontrollable gay son, Shelley, were surely written in hell."   --Buddy Hamilton

"**Blood Moon** reads like *Dynasty* on steroids. A compelling psycho-sexual adventure of three beautiful men meeting on the fast road to hell."   -Kathryn Cobb

"**Blood Moon** is like reading Anaïs Nin on Viagra with a bump of crystal meth."
          --Eugene Raymond, one-time book reviewer for AFTER DARK MAGAZINE

MIDNIGHT IN SAVANNAH

BY **DARWIN PORTER**   ISBN 09668030-1-9   Paperback   **$14.95**

This is the more explicit, and more entertaining, alternative to John Berendt's Savannah-based *Midnight in the Garden of Good and Evil.* Bemused but decadent, it's a saga of corruption, greed, sexual tension, and murder that gets down and dirty in the Deep Old South. For more than a year, after its publication in 2000, it was one of the best-selling counterculture novels in Georgia and the Carolinas, as defined by sales figures from the South's then-leading gay book-store, Outwrite Books (Atlanta). Newspapers throughout the South, both gay and straight, editorialized on this, the book that satirized THE BOOK that changed the face of tourism in Savannah for all time.

"In Darwin Porter's <u>Midnight,</u> both Lavender Morgan ("At 72, the world's oldest courtesan") and Tipper Zelda ("an obese, fading chanteuse taunted as "the black widow,") purchase lust from sexually conflicted young men with drop-dead faces, chiseled bodies, and genetically gift-ed crotches. These women once relied on their physicality to steal the hearts and fortunes of the world's richest and most powerful men. Now, as they slide closer every day to joining the corpses of their former husbands, these once-beautiful women must depend, in a perverse twist of fate, on sexual outlaws for <u>le petit mort.</u> And to survive, the hustlers must idle their person-al dreams while struggling to cajole what they need from a sexual liaison they detest. Mendacity reigns, Perversity in extremis. Physical beauty as living hell. CAT ON A HOT TIN ROOF'S Big Daddy must be spinning in his grave right now."

---EUGENE RAYMOND, FORMER CRITIC FOR **AFTER DARK** MAGAZINE

In Hollywood at the Dawn of the Talkies, most of the sins were never shown on film

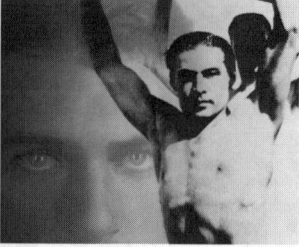

Hollywood's Silent Closet

by Darwin Porter

A scandalous new info-novel where 90% of every story is true.
"A brilliant primer for the *Who's Who* of early Hollywood"
(Gay London Times)

"Intricately researched by ex-entertainment columnist Darwin Porter,
this is the most realistic account ever written about sex,
murder, blackmail, and degradation in early Hollywood."

A banquet of information about the pansexual intrigues of Hollywood between 1919 and 1926, compiled from eyewitness interviews with men and women, all of them insiders, who flourished in its midst. Not for the timid, it names names, and doesn't spare the guilty... If you believe, like Truman Capote, that the literary treatment of gossip will become the literature of the 21st century, then you will love this book.

From the Georgia Literary Association
(an affiliate of Blood Moon Productions)

ISBN 0966-8030-2-7   746 pages, 60 vintage photos. $24.95